Bad Boys
and Tough Tattoos
A Social History of the Tattoo
with Gangs, Sailors
and Street-Corner Punks
1950-1965

"This is no mere book for tattoo buffs, nor is it only on tattooing. It's for a far larger audience of readers who may be ready to accompany the author right into the Anchor Tattoo Shop—with all its dangers, pathos, and bathos—for close-up views of a large segment of young men seldom mentioned (let alone so well portrayed) in any other context. An what a guide! Nobody could do it better than Sam Steward."
Wardell B. Pomeroy, PhD, Co-author of the *Kinsey Reports*
(From the Foreword)

"An admirable piece of anthropological research; [Steward] lived within his 'tribe', scrutinized it with an acutely perceptive eye, and reported his findings in clear and concise narrative. He leads the reader into a special underworld known to few and makes it vividly alive and realistic. Any student of human behavior or anyone interested in the diversity of human life will profit from this fascinating book."
Paul H. Gebhard, PhD, formerly Director, Institute for Sex Research
(the Kinsey Institute), and Professor Emeritus of Anthropology,
Indiana University, Bloomington, Indiana

"Sam Steward has always had a knack for getting close to people, both to his own and to their great enjoyment. . . . The marvel is, as this book shows, that he opens doors and 'tunes in' just as easily at the lowest and roughest social levels—where his personal tone and his tattoo talents, not his erudition, cut the ice. He opens many views to us all of the obvious and the hidden sexual motivations in this strange land."
C. A. Tripp, PhD, Director, Psychological Research Associates, Inc.,
Nyack, New York; Author of *The Homosexual Matrix*

Bad Boys
and Tough Tattoos
A Social History of the Tattoo with Gangs, Sailors and Street-Corner Punks 1950-1965

Samuel M. Steward, PhD

Harrington Park Press
New York • London

ISBN 0-918393-76-0

Published by

Harrington Park Press, 10 Alice Street, Binghamton, NY 13904-1580
EUROSPAN/Haworth, 3 Henrietta Street, London WC2E 8LU England

Harrington Park Press is a subsidiary of The Haworth Press, Inc., 10 Alice Street, Binghamton, New York 13904-1580.

Cover design by John Paul Lona

Library of Congress Cataloging-in-Publication Data

Steward, Samuel M.
    Bad boys and tough tattoos : a social history of the tattoo with gangs, sailors, and street-corner punks, 1950-1965 / Samuel M. Steward.
       p. cm.
    Includes bibliographical references and index.
    ISBN 0-918393-76-0 (alk. paper)
    1. Steward, Samuel M. 2. Tattoo artists—United States—Biography. 3. Tattooing—Psychological aspects. 4. Tattooing—Social aspects. I. Title.
GT5960.T36S747   1990b
391'.65'0973—dc20   90-33832
                                                       CIP

For
Dr. C. A. Tripp
Mover and Shaker

CONTENTS

ABOUT THE AUTHOR

Samuel M. Steward, PhD, was a tattoo artist in Chicago and Oakland — under the name of Phil Sparrow — for 18 years. Prior to that, he was a university professor of English for 20 years. A contributor to *World Book Encyclopedia* and the author of several hundred stories that have appeared in European magazines, Dr. Steward has also published many books, including *The Caravaggio Shawl* (Alyson, 1989), *Murder Is Murder Is Murder* (Alyson, 1984), *Parisian Lives* (St. Martin's, 1984), *Chapters From an Autobiography* (Grey Fox, 1981), and *Dear Sammy: Letters From Gertrude Stein and Alice B. Toklas, With a Memior* (Houghton, 1977). He has also written several erotic novels under the pseudonym Phil Andros, including *Different Strokes* (Perineum, 1984), *The Boys in Blue* (Perineum, 1984), and *Below the Belt and Other Stories* (Perineum, 1981).

Bad Boys
and Tough Tattoos
A Social History of the Tattoo
with Gangs, Sailors
and Street-Corner Punks
1950-1965

Foreword

It has been my pleasure to have known Sam Steward for forty years, more or less, and to have spent many hours with him in his shop watching him "operate." This was sometimes done with Dr. Alfred Kinsey, and sometimes alone or with other members of the Institute for Sex Research. Sam also would, on occasion, wrench himself away from his fascinating job in Chicago and travel southward 225 miles to visit us at the Institute. It was also my pleasure to see him several times at his California location—this long after Dr. Kinsey's untimely death. In fact, I knew Sam just before he took his plunge into tattoodling, as he was wont to call it. It never ceased to amaze me how he was able to transform himself from the academic ivory-towered English professor to an entrepreneur who could handle very sticky situations and some very tough customers with an aplomb that even those raised in lower social levels would find difficult to duplicate.

Of course, I had known about Sam's journal from the moment of its inception—the one that he had started at Kinsey's request, to try to discover the sexual motivations for getting tattooed—and as each installment was sent to the Institute, I read it with fascination and even incredulity. If I had not seen with my own eyes how he operated in his Chicago shop, I think parts of it would have made me wonder if he were not gilding the lily a bit. I can assure you, however, that the only lilies he has gilded were on the bodies of his customers.

I am reminded of an old story about a man running for sheriff in a small Southern county. A proposed law limiting the hunting of squirrels was soon to come to a vote there. He was asked whether he favored the law. His reply was: "Half of mah constituents are for this here law and half are agin it. As fer me, I'm fer mah constituents."

I feel the same way about tattooing. I'm neither fer it nor agin it, but I *am* for understanding the tattooist, the tattooee, and the entire phenomenon so well revealed in this book.

Tattooing never held any particular interest for me until I began interviewing lower-social-level males, particularly males in prison. Here I was constantly running across tattooed men. Their nonchalance and even indifference about their tattooed skin made me realize that here was another distinction between them and the protected college-level people with whom I was used to dealing. At first timidly and then more boldly, I would ask them about their tattoos and the meanings they had for their possessors. When Sam came on our horizon, we realized that here was a golden opportunity to secure some answers that could be more than mere speculations. As a scientist I might have wished for a more statistical analysis, especially in Part V, but there are many roads that lead to Rome. The road Sam has taken gives us a "feel" of the situation, as well as the "feel" of a most remarkable individual whose biography needs to see the light of day. Who better to tell it than the master craftsman himself?

This is no mere book for tattoo buffs, nor is it concerned only with tattooing. It's for a far larger audience of readers who may be ready to accompany the author right into the Anchor Tattoo Shop — with all its dangers, pathos, and bathos — for close-up views of a large segment of young men seldom mentioned (let alone so well portrayed) in any other context. And what a guide! Nobody could do it better than Sam Steward.

— Wardell B. Pomeroy, PhD
[Co-author of the *Kinsey Reports*]

Introduction

In the early 1950s I abandoned a career of twenty years of university teaching to become a tattoo artist.

Today in the 1990s such a statement would not cause much stir, save for an eyebrow lifted here and there at the wide gulf between the two occupations, but forty years ago it was startling. At about the same time I left the tower of Academe, a professor in New England forsook his career to join a circus, and *Life* magazine carried a large sensational story about it. I was also approached for an account of my "treachery," but since any publicity would have embarrassed my sister and her husband socially — and perhaps in a business sense — I was forced to decline.

Dr. Alfred Kinsey, however, founder of the sex research institute at Indiana University, suggested that I keep a daily journal to see what might be learned about the sexual motivations for getting tattooed. I did, and the account was continued for about six years under his skillful prodding and encouragement. It went on even after his death. By the time it was abandoned it had reached mammoth proportions, filling several large volumes of typescript. The present account is drawn from that record, which in its complete form exists in the archives of the Kinsey Institute at Indiana University.

"You have a unique opportunity," he said. "Not only have you had some training in scientific observation, you are probably one of the half-dozen literate tattoo artists in the country. This is too good a chance to miss. Who knows? It may become a source-book for psychologists and psychiatrists and social workers — and for the Institute for Sex Research," he added with a certain wry humor.

His interests in the sexual implications and motivations of tattooing, which he suspected and sought confirmation for, are heavily reflected here. The deeper the involvement with tattooing grew, the more it became evident that in one way or another more than three-quarters of the tattoos applied were put on because of some aspect of sexual motivation.

But there was more in my journal than the discovery of the twenty-five sexual motivations for tattooing. It became a partial record of segments of the subcultures that existed in the 1950s. The tattoo shop was of course a natural magnet for the very young boot sailors stationed at nearby Great Lakes Naval Training Station, but it also drew into it the youth gangs of Chicago, the juvenile delinquents, the sexually confused and rootless (sometimes illiterate) young men — the rebels without causes. In a sense the journal crystallized a troubled time that included McCarthyism, Korea, and the seeds of the deeper rebellion of the 1960s with its spreading contagions of free speech, more liberal thought, and permissive sex.

How to present this information, this bubble of time, was troubling. If it were couched in academic gobbledegook or the pseudo-scientific terminology of which would-be lay-experts and phony intellectuals considered themselves the informed masters, hundreds of anecdotes and illustrative materials would have to vanish. They would seem misplaced or frivolous in a scholarly work. Alice Toklas once suggested that I should let the "weight of the anecdotes carry the thing." I have tried to do this.

The result is not a history of tattooing nor a roster of tattoo artists. There is a brief historical sketch in Appendix A, and an incomplete note on tattoo literature in Appendix B. Nor is this a "how-to" book about the techniques of tattooing; the remarks about methods could easily be completely removed without damaging the main intent of the book. And it is perhaps the only volume on tattooing not dependent on tattoo photographs to boost sales.

The book is completely subjective. There is no intention to retell the old stories, to perpetuate past myths or errors, to upgrade the "art" of tattooing, nor to make more dense the fog of the mystique around it. Everything herein comes from direct observation, and many readers will find much of the mystery and folklore of tattooing is removed.

A direct chronological formula marks the early part, making it seem almost like an autobiography, as an attempt is made to explain the underlying reasons for my disgust with and departure from university life. But after that, do not expect the arrangement and symmetry of the scholar's monograph. The order, logic, and design of the universe cannot be impressed on the chaos of life as it was observed on the skidrow of South State Street in Chicago.

Permit me to make a kind of blanket apology. Whenever a deduction is reached, an inference drawn, or a generalization advanced, imagine that one of these phrases stands in front of it: "It would seem to me —," or "In my opinion —," or "I believe that —." Thus all sociological, medical, or psychiatric criticism of my observations may be turned away. For after all — what does a tattoo artist know when put alongside the professionals, the men of genius?

PART I

From Academia to Skidrow

For about twenty years of my life I had been a professor of English, teaching at various universities in the West and Midwest, finally ending in Chicago at a small, peculiar church school, a kind of co-ed religious kindergarten staffed with mediocrities and trumpeting a reputation which was founded more on its basketball team than on scholarly aims and accomplishments. At best it was a sort of protective nursing school where parents sent teenagers until they were old enough to go to work. The North Central Association of universities was continually hounding it because it had no endowment — and when it did manage to raise some money, it built an alumni auditorium for its basketball team rather than a new library.

The student body of the early 1950s was cowed, clannish, and conformist. It was drawn from lower and middle-class backgrounds which were narrowly parochial. Every member of the university's English department occasionally had to take charge of an entering freshman class. In my opening session with such a group one year I asked a series of rapid questions trying to find out how much the students knew. Not one of the forty-odd boys and girls had ever heard of Homer, but in the same group thirty-four of them knew how to change a spark-plug. Out of approximately two hundred and fifty students who sat in my classes each year, possibly three or four grew to be "illuminated" or liberalized. The curtain went up for them on a world of art, music, or literature. The others were content with TV, beer, and sex — and an eventual progress into the world of work, of getting up at six every morning and going to work to make enough money to buy enough food to get enough energy to get up and go to work to earn enough money . . . and so on.

Those few students in whose eyes the light began to shine were not much reward for the teacher. The pay was small. Whatever "prestige" came from being a university professor could not be banked. You had to decide whether to take a taxi in the rain or to save the money for a haircut. Some strange immorality made the university raise the salary for each new child a married teacher produced. Bachelors—like myself, even with our advanced degrees—went on at the same old level.

During the last years of this harrowing life things got worse. I grew to loathe the matrix which imprisoned me. On some mornings I had to take a benzedrine tablet to face the doltish students. But what else to do? All my life I had made a living with my brain, and it had brought me little. At some point in the last three years of teaching, the seed of my rebellion broke and the spores went spinning along the blood. It was a mid-life crisis, undoubtedly. Ben Hecht spoke of Sherwood Anderson's break with his past and the writing it produced as "the wistful idealization of the masculine menopause." My menopause turned me down a decidedly materialistic channel.

Tattooing had really never entered my awareness very much. When it did, the associations were always with sailors first, ex-convicts second, and various toughs and gangsters last. In the 1920s I had read in some obscure novel about the three signs of "badness"—socks rolled down to the ankle, long sideburns, and a tattoo showing on the wrist. Robert Mitchum's demented killer had *Love* and *Hate* tattooed on the fingers of each hand. There was a radio program which ended with descriptions of wanted criminals; invariably their tattoos were described. A Marlboro cigarette campaign popularized a man with a crudely drawn eagle or anchor on the back of his hand.

Perhaps, then, the first tangible sign of my "anti-intellectual" revolt was that I got a small tattoo very high on my left deltoid. This was an odd experience for me.

I had been "supering" with all kinds of companies that came to Chicago—ballet, opera, operetta like *The Student Prince*, and dramatic like *Diamond Lil*, carrying a spear or otherwise being in one of the crowd scenes demanded by the production. The fat and white-haired homosexual who was the entrepreneur for the "supers" called on me often, and gradually my status grew until certain definite roles were assigned to me for the troupes that needed extras. In *Scheherazade* with the old Ballets Russes de Monte Carlo I was a guardian eunuch in the first scene; in *Gaîté Parisienne* a member of the small on-stage orchestra; in *Carmen* one of the townspeople, and later a smuggler.

In the Ballet Russe version of *The Nutcracker* I was always the gondolier who in the last scene rowed across the stage the gondola from which the little girl heroine descended after her journey to the land of make-believe. For this the Ballet Russe furnished me with a gondolier's costume, a part of which was a knit sleeveless dark-green nylon shirt.

It occurred to me that a gondolier might very well have a small anchor on his shoulder, the one facing the audience, to go with the large gold ear-ring in his left ear. The idea of getting the anchor tattooed on me was both fascinating and terrifying. Accordingly, one rainy night before that year's arrival of the Ballets Russes, I fortified myself with a couple of drinks and went down to south State Street in Chicago to get one.

I got it, all right—from "Tatts" Thomas, a skinny baldheaded man with a mustache, the ends of which were waxed to long fine points. The sensation hurt like hell—at times burning, at other times like a knife of ice. When it was done he slapped a piece of brown wrapping paper on it, secured the paper with scotch tape, and told me to keep it dry.

This is a very superficial account of my getting a first tattoo, for in those early days the motivations were not very clear. There were undoubtedly deeper currents at work, but at the moment I could not see them. Many of my friends were horrified and shocked. "Why in the world would you want to do a thing like that?" was the question most often asked.

Why, indeed?

No one of my academic colleagues was tattooed, as far as I knew, so it was hardly possible for them to understand. I soon discovered that whenever I mentioned my anchor to other friends, I was at once furnished with many reasons why they would not ever consider getting tattooed. Most of these friends at this time were homosexual, and in the 1950s there seemed to be a particular horror of tattoos among them.

Take Paul's reaction, for instance. Paul, a slight balding male, was a ribbon-clerk at Marshall Field's department store. "Really," he said, "to be quite honest about it, I just couldn't stand the pain."

Fear of pain is a universal reaction. An injection in a doctor's office makes many persons weak; the prospect of hundreds of thousands of pricks over a period of minutes is enough to turn anyone white. The mere sight of needles can make a truckdriver faint in anticipation. Everyone who has been in the armed forces has seen draftees keel over in line as they approach the needle. The subconscious says in effect: "Let's get out of here!" and sends a large supply of blood to the leg muscles to prepare for flight. And when the blood leaves the head, the person faints. Paul resisted all my reassurances that the speed of the machines made the individual pricks merge together, so that the sensation was that of heat or cold. "Not for me," he said, shaking his head.

Or take Bruce. "Me get tattooed?" he said scornfully. "Never! That's too low-class for me."

That was the feeling of many young arrogant males, largely of the middle class. Possibly they were right about their status being lowered by a tattoo. TV, movies, and newspapers had imprinted on the public mind the connection between tattoos and criminal or derelict behavior.

Two reactions seem to be possible in persons who see a tattoo on someone. One is complete fascination, a feeling that here is the ultimate stud, the great macho, the sexual satyr, the Marlboro man, the far-traveling sailor, the incomparable sadistic master, the Genet criminal just released from prison. The other is a complete revulsion: the tattoo represents the epitome of sleaze, of low-class background, of cheap vulgarity and bad taste, everything that intelligence and sophistication have conditioned you to despise. To persons of this second view, it is useless to mention the tattoos of the late King of Denmark or the Duke of Windsor, Burt Lancaster, Sean Connery, Admiral Halsey, Senator Goldwater, George Schultz, and many others.

Allan's reaction was different. "I wouldn't want anything permanently on me," he said petulantly. "I'm sure I'd get tired of *any* design that I had to wear forever. Besides, there's the fact that you can be so easily identified by them."

"Thinking of taking up a life of crime?" I asked. "Are you

planning ahead for the day when you'll do chop off someone's head?'' Later on I was to discover that many pseudo-bad boys refused to get tattooed for this same fear of easy identification, whereas the real criminal types seemed almost eager to flaunt their tattoos in defiance of authority.

Then there was Clifton, a Long Island snob of the first water. ''In my family,'' he said, ''well—the men in my family have always admired Brooks Brothers' suits, for example, because of their absolute purity of line. No decoration, no frills. Such plainness is the mark of good taste. So quite naturally I'm against tattooing. It's decoration, and that's in bad taste.''

I nodded, watching him twirl a large amethyst ring on his finger which seemed to me to be in the worst possible taste. In those days we used to call such baubles ''bitch badges.''

And there was Ralph, a weightlifter and hustler. ''Chee, no,'' he said. ''I ain't never gonna get tattooed. Dat'd spoil me and I'd lose points when dey judge duh contests.'' But Axel, another weightlifter, was covered down to the waist. ''I think when you're decorated you look purtier,'' he said.

Here were two different narcissists speaking: one so admired his unmarked skin that he shied from tattoos; the other, a pseudo-narcissist, made the mistake of feeling that tattoos would make him even more attractive—an error which he discovered for himself after losing many contests because of his markings.

Clifton, the snob, made another point which was curiously interesting. ''I am afraid of tattoos,'' he said, ''because of the sexual expression involved.'' In those early days my own knowledge had not taken me far enough into the subterranean world of tattooing to understand what he meant: whether a tattoo revealed his own nature along narcissistic or sado-masochistic lines, or whether he might be sexually aroused while being tattooed. Albert Parry, one of the early Freudians to write about tattooing, definitely compared it to a sexual act, with both an active and a passive partner, the insertion of fluid (inks) under the skin, and so on.

* * * * *

Having told some of my friends and university colleagues—more for shock value than anything else—that I was thinking of becoming a tattoo artist, I felt that the time had come to do something about it. I bought a correspondence course in tattooing from the "only school of its kind in existence," a poorly mimeographed set of lessons each bound in orange paper. The material seemed fascinating at the moment, but hindsight reveals that it was not at all informative, and that the "Professor" who wrote it — a Milton Zeis of Rockford, Illinois — knew very little about tattooing. The lessons were extremely dull, or at least it seemed so from my frosty pinnacle of a Ph.D. in English literature and an oft-repeated course in life-drawing at the Art Institute in Chicago.

But the tattoo lessons were all finished faithfully, even down to practicing alphabets and lettering. Zeis later told me that I was the only one who had ever finished the course. He was only a merchant, not a tattooist, and his course was made up of everything that the con-men tattooists told him.

Learning to tattoo from a book is just about as successfully accomplished as learning to swim from a book in your living-room. I did learn some things about machines and inks, and mastered various mechanical aspects. But it was not until I began to go to Dietzel, the old master in Milwaukee, that I really learned how to tattoo. Tattooing seems to be one of the few remaining skills that must be passed from a master to an apprentice.

My life suddenly seemed to draw together. Why had I been studying drawing for the past four years? Why had I been using an electric vibro-tool to make designs on metal? Was not tattooing the farthest distance I could get from the academic world? It was as if the broad, fan-like spread of my existence had come to a focus, indeed, taken on a funnel shape, and I was sliding down into a world of which I knew absolutely nothing.

The life ahead of me was as different from the one I had known as benedictine is from cheap red wine. Up until now there had been a good lot of the intellectual snob in me. I had had two books published, neither of which in any way interrupted my comfortable obscurity. I had been an encyclopedia editor. I had traveled widely in Europe, and visited Gertrude Stein and Alice Toklas several times, both at their chateau at Bilignin in the south of France and at their Paris apartment on the rue Christine. I had corresponded with Thomas Mann and lunched with his family in Küsnacht. I had met and become friendly with André Gide, Jean Cocteau, and Julien

Green in Paris, and been intimate with Thornton Wilder, and was later to detail such things (and write more novels under the name of Phil Andros) in an autobiography. My talents and ambitions were so negligible that they never took me into inner circles, but had enabled me to enjoy myself on the periphery of the literary world.

More might have been accomplished had I not been trapped like a djinni in the bottle — the liquor bottle. It took many years and many painful experiences to climb out of it. But it was accomplished with the help of a group of happy ex-drunks in the old Watertower group in Chicago, which included several radio and TV personalities, and both the mother and father of a then-rising young male movie star. None of us had a sturdy enough belief in religion to help us break the shell of narcissism that surrounds all alcoholics, but we could agree that booze itself was a "power greater than ourselves."

In André Gide's *Les Nourritures Terrestres* there was a striking idea which many years before had lodged itself firmly in my memory. He said that at least once in one's life a total break should be made, no matter from what — home town, family, room, or thought — but the separation should be absolute. He carried this thought farther than I could, however, convinced as he was that his desire should become his law, and that he should turn himself into the most "irreplaceable of human beings."

I could not be as positive as he was, since I was uncertain of my own powers. My ego said no. Even after I made my break with Academia, it was not total. For quite a while I went on teaching during the days, and tattooing on weekends. It was a strange and disturbing overlapping.

It astonished me that in this renunciation — or quest — I began to seek the opposites of things I had long admired. In the tattoo shop I commenced to wear the oldest and "toughest" clothes possible, levis or Navy dungarees and a leather jacket, changing to them after I left the university and as soon as I arrived downtown. In those days there were no leather-shops; I had to get my jacket from Sears. My anchor tattoo — and two small ones experimentally self-applied — began to ally me with the toughs, the herd, the skidrow bums — all those who revolted against the "establishment." But if my hatred of my matrix was genuine, and I really wanted to expel myself from it, what better way to start than with tattoos, and tattooing — certainly as anti-social as anything I could find? Was I bent on self-destruction — or just bored? I'd settle the question myself. I felt I needed no help.

The "street" — that skidrow where I was later to work — had the kind of atmosphere that bred disaster. You could almost breathe it in the air, and I was lucky that I was not more sensitive, or my preliminary wanderings down there would have crushed and stifled me. As it was, my empathic reaction had to be kept under rigid control by maintaining what the aestheticians call "psychic distance." But I still had the sensation of sinking down into it. It became increasingly difficult to hoist myself back to the university level again. The street's miasma and excitement began to play hob with my sense of reality, giving me an almost schizoid separation in my mind and emotions.

Formerly I had considered myself less sheltered and more sophisticated than my colleagues at the university. Yeah, I had known the "great world," or so I believed. The shock that came when I actually descended into the world of the honky-tonk of south State Street in Chicago was extremely violent. I found I had known very little of life until then . . . the seamy, sodden world of whores and pimps and pushers and winos and con-men — yes, and of tattoo artists.

*　*　*　*　*

Zeis sold me not only the correspondence course but a few machines and some colors, and the experimental period began. I even had some business cards printed: extraordinary ones, announcing that "Professor Philip Sparrow" would tattoo "Anything You Want — Anywhere" but "By Appointment Only," and gave my telephone number. The pen-name — or needle-name, if you will — had to be chosen because I was still teaching at the university. Something told me it would not be exactly politic to let it be known in the "cloister" that I was embarking upon this unusual adventure.

The name of Phil Sparrow came from an obscure poem by John Skelton entitled *Boke of Phyllippe Sparrowe*, a sixteenth century elegy on the death of a pet bird which had belonged to fair Jane Scroupe. It had always appealed to me because of its ribaldry, its echoes of Catullus, and its hodgepodge of buffoonery and charm —

a rough sketch of the sort of thing that Rabelais carried to a high point, a satiric lament for the death of a lady's pet sparrow which had been trained to pick crumbs from her cleavage. Later I would feel that it was a lucky choice, for in a sense I would be picking crumbs for Kinsey . . .

One of the cards fell into the hands of a much-tattooed ex-merchant seaman (or so he claimed). He was a really compulsive tattoo buff, the first of many later met. His name was Larry. He was small, about five feet two, and was all tied up inside in what Alice Toklas used to call "little blue French knots." He had a dozen rationalizations for being so heavily tattooed. It was he who actually started me on the path.

He telephoned me one day. "I've just heard," he said, "that old Mickey Kellett has got all the tattoo gear of Mel Nelson, a sword-swallower who just died, and he wants to sell it. Design sheets and machines and stencils and everything. A bargain."

"How much does he want?" I asked.

"Thirty-five bucks," said Larry. "He's down at the Fleetwood, a flophouse at 624 South State. Whyncha go down and see him?"

"Maybe I will," I said.

I thought about it for a day, and then I got out an old skimpy trenchcoat, put on my oldest rain-hat, and went down to the Fleetwood Hotel.

It was a real flophouse. The dirty halls smelled of stale urine and beer overridden by a harsh carbolic disinfectant. The cashier's desk was wire-enclosed. The cubicles themselves were green-painted plywood partitions not extending to the ceiling, but with chicken wire over the tops to cut down on the thieving. Grumbling, the cashier went to knock on Kellett's door and finally roused him from his winey stupor.

There was a kind of old-fashioned gentility and politeness to Mickey Kellett when he got himself awake. He seemed a very gentle man, a sort of half-dopey drunk. He opened a small trunk to show me Nelson's gear. When he raised the lid, the bitter acid stench of old acetate and just plain filth was overpowering.

"Needs a lot of clean-up," old Mickey said, his dead-white jowls trembling a little.

"Sure does," I said.

Here were the implements of the "jagger's" (a very derogatory term) trade at its worst — old instruments wrapped in dirty rags, and the machines themselves coated with accumulations of inks and grease to a depth of a quarter-inch. There were many dirty ancient carnival design-boards — "flash" as Kellett called them — the first time I had heard the word. One day such "flash" might be museum pieces, or perhaps they already were. There were eight machines in various states of disrepair, a transformer and a rheostat, and hundreds of ancient stencils, all coated with greasy smearings of vaseline and black powder. The drawings were very poorly executed, and yet there was a kind of primitive charm to them. Would anyone really put such hideous designs on human skin?

Kellett was quite a talker, although I had a feeling that his slow gentle voice belied the sort of person he really was. Showing me the designs that Nelson had made but had not yet colored in, he said, "And Mel's sure not gonna color 'em from the graveyard."

Then he rambled on about tattooing. "Wotthehell," he said. "Why work? You can make a good livin' this way. Set up at Riverview Park, or better still, go to that little arcade at Belmont and the Elevated and hang up your flash and get a needle buzzin', and they'll come all the way out there just to find you."

"That's not a very good location," I said. "How could you make any money there?"

He shook his head. "M'boy," he said. "I had a worse location than that in 1942 and I made eleven grand that year." He rummaged among some papers in a suitcase and came up with a much-thumbed day-book. "Here," he said. "Looky-here — I made as high as $77 a day that year."

End result: I bought the whole lot, and managed to get it home. From that day I was hooked. It took a week to clean all the junk and remove the wiring and needle holders from the footlocker. I scrubbed every stencil with detergent. They still stank.

The meeting with Mickey Kellett stuck in my mind. It was a strangely saddening experience — this aging feeble man, fighting the idea of failure, keeping up a kind of front, and scoffing at those who attempted conventional ways to earn their living.

My friends looked on these newly acquired treasures and were fascinated, especially by the ancient "flash," tin-bound on the edges and crudely drawn, strung together with wire so that Nelson—or "Mephisto" as he called himself—could hang them up quickly when the carnival opened. At that time the boards were not yet considered collector's items, and they were gradually given away to friends. There was a two-foot high stack of them, hundreds of sketches, rather attractive relics of a vanishing mediocre American art-form, in the same class of disappearing rarities as Egyptian fortune-telling machines, peep-show viewers, player-pianos, cable cars, and buggy-whips.

Could I have seen all the eighteen years ahead suddenly unrolled in their complexity, I might never have plunged into the tattoo world. It would have frightened the hell out of me. As it was, I remember thinking as I taxied north on that dark and rainy March afternoon with Mephisto's odorous trunk at my feet: "There are odd dark caverns ahead."

And there were, indeed.

PART II

A Cut-Throat World

A few months went by, and it was summer. In the midst of a lazy sunbath one day I remembered old Mickey Kellett and once more heard him saying "Why work? Get yourself a little hole in the wall, hang up your flash, and you can spend the rest of your life enjoying yourself."

In talking about this new enthusiasm of tattooing to my friends I had been saying ". . . and then when I retire from teaching I'll go to some seaport town like San Francisco and set up my shop, and spend the rest of my life putting designs on sailors." But my secret embarrassment over the whole matter led me to denigrate the skill by usually referring to it as "tattoodling" or some other form of the word: tattoodles, tattoodler — as if to show my "intellectual" scorn of such a profession.

The new extension to the statement of Mickey Kellett was simply — why wait until I'm sixty-five? At most I might then have five years before the fingers clamp down with arthritis, or like Milton you sit clutching at your faded eyes. Why not give up this rat-race of teaching, this hopeless and profitless dealing with dullness, and stop it all in your forties?

Caught in the web of this day-dream, I filled it in from all angles. I'd have a modern aseptic shop. A window with signs and lettering: "Have that tattoo now. Fire-reds, sea-blues, hot yellows . . ." Perhaps there would be a sort of museum as well, with ancient tattoo equipment and flash from the nineteenth century. And then suddenly, shifting, the idea of Paris or Hong Kong . . . "American Tattoodling . . . Le Tatouage américain. Toutes couleurs — fières, violentes, et foncées. Consultation gratuite . . ."

To look back now on such impractical fantasies is indeed amusing, but their very naiveté shows my ignorance then of the realities of the subject. Revealed also is the dramatically great power of the mystique of tattooing. From that June afternoon on I felt that nothing would stop me.

Fall came, and winter. And one day there was another phone call from Larry, the tattooed ex-merchant mariner. By this time I had put on about a dozen tattoos, most of the "victims" brought to my apartment by Larry. The Zeis correspondence course said that you should practice tattooing on Idaho potatoes, or on grapefruit with the yellow peeled off but the white pith remaining. I tried a potato once and then forgot to throw it away. My aunt boiled it and when it was peeled, a rough head of Christ was exposed on the white skin. She nearly fainted, thinking there had been a Visitation . . .

Potatoes and grapefruit were a part of Zeis's folklore. There was nothing suitable for practice except skin. So some of my friends and a few of my enemies bear early Sparrow work. It is more or less gratifying to see that it has held up fairly well, even after all the intervening years.

Larry's phone call concerned the people who ran one of the oldest arcades on south State Street. They were faced with a problem. They had a tattoo artist working there who was a confirmed drunk, a real "jagger" doing bad work, being dirty and filthy and infecting customers, sitting surrounded by his empty pint muscatel bottles. ("They counted twenty-one empties one morning," Larry said. "And he spits on the floor an' they even caught him pissin' in the corner once.")

"Tsk," I said.

"So the guy that runs it for the owner," Larry said, "told me that they gotta get a new tattoo artist and I told him I knew one, and he said come on down and see him. You wanna go?"

"You know I'm teaching," I said. "I can't stop that."

"You could do it part-time," Larry said. "C'mon, let's go see them. I'll go with you."

It was November by them, a slushy dirty day in 1952, dark and threatening snow again, when I met Larry at the south end of the Loop in Chicago, and we started down the "street." I had not been that far south on State Street since I had stopped drinking. There were arcades with tattoo joints in most of them, and burlesque shows, pawn shops, stores selling cheap clothing, and flophouses, one after the other. Our goal was the Sportland Arcade, three blocks down; and with each block the neighborhood grew more shabby. South State Street had been an embarrassment for many years, not only to the City Council but to the elegant merchants like Marshall Field's and Carson's who were on upper State Street. This honky-tonk section, with the Pacific Garden Mission and the stewbums, the bottles in doorways and the dried urine streamstains on the sidewalks, was a real skidrow—number three in size in Chicago, as I later discovered. The regulars of the State Street skidrow felt themselves vastly superior in status to the bums of West Madison or North Clark streets.

By the time we had gone two blocks I was ready to turn back.

"Larry," I said, "I don't know whether I can go through with this."

"Aw c'mon," he said. "It's not much farther. It ain't really so bad."

We finally reached the Sportland Arcade. It was the shabbiest of all. The other arcades had at least looked modern—glass fronts and lots of fluorescent lighting and bright new pinball machines, lunch counters and fine glass doors. The Sportland looked dead and dingy from the outside, and darker and deader inside—long and gloomy, with dirty walls. An ancient V-for-Victory neon sign, a relic of World War II, hung unlighted from the cracked and stained ceiling. Against the left wall, running clear back to a shooting gallery, was a tightly packed row of vintage stereopticon peepshow machines, the kind into which you dropped a nickel or a dime and then peered through binocular lenses to watch a dozen pictures drop one after the other. These antique machines dated from the 1920s, and the girls—the "models" they contained, were the unattractive hoydenish skags of the early jazz and flapper era. Down the center of the arcade ran a double row of the same kind of machines. In one corner was a dusty player piano, and another "orchestral" piano, both with "Out of Order" signs hung on them. A glass-enclosed Egyptian fortune-telling painted plaster lady with a rotting veil peered at a row of cards; her hand moved over them, wheels whirred, and your printed fortune dropped into a slot—all for a dime.

Built against the right-hand wall was what looked like a small three-sided construction shack with a slanting roof. The front side was open, but was dark and empty. An extendable baby-gate closed it off from the public. It was about nine feet square.

"There's the shop," Larry said.

I gulped. The musty smell, the rough wooden floors, the general air of dinginess—it was almost too much. "C'mon back," Larry said, "and I'll introduce you to Frank."

Frank was a handsome six-foot broad-shouldered Lithuanian with sleek heavy dark brown hair and eyes that were coldly appraising. His nose was a bit large for his excellent face with its high cheekbones, but he had good lips and a strong chin. He was a sexy-looking stud with a kind of steel-trap alertness to his stance and movements. Charisma dripped from him; his aura suggested nights of tumult and lust. I later learned he had been a rum-runner at the age of fifteen, and later a professional boxer, a grocery store owner, a forest ranger, a pimp, a seller of dirty books (the popular eight-pagers of the times) and dirtier pictures, manager and bouncer in a whorehouse, and now a penny-arcade. He also showed dirty movies (this was long before Supreme Court liberation) in one special peepshow machine he had rigged up—at $3.00 per viewing; his clientele was large, and the movies changed every week. This later proved his downfall—but of course I knew nothing of all this at that first meeting.

There was another guy who ran the shooting gallery—Denny, a heavily tattooed ex-cop and ex-bartender from Dayton, Ohio, a rotund fat man with a 54-inch waist. He ran the gallery and also the left wall of peepshow machines. His size and weight made him well qualified for the job of bouncer, which he often exercised with great glee.

Larry introduced me to Frank. I never learned exactly what Larry had told him about my teaching background or sexual orientation; Frank never spoke of it but he undoubtedly knew all. I explained that I already had a job, that I could not work more than part-time.

"Okay," Frank said. "You come down here Friday nights and Saturday and Sunday, and maybe Wednesday if you want, and you can make a buck if you do good work. We can let that old drunk sonofabitch have it the rest of the time so's he won't get too mad."

"What about the pay?"

"Hah!" said Frank. "Old Mister Perry who owns the joint wants thirty-five percent for himself, and the rest of it's yours. I might as well tell you—if Randy turns in five percent he's doin' good. That's all up to you. You can be honest if you want to." And he winked.

"Will Randy be mad at me?" I asked. "I don't want to start off in this business by makin' enemies."

Frank shrugged. "Sure, he'll be pissed off," he said. "But we've told him a thousand times he's gotta straighten up or we'll kick his ass outa here. Mister Perry wants him all the way out. I can promise you there won't be no trouble."

So it was arranged. Then we went to look at the shop. Frank turned on the light. It was a dirty shop of the kind which could bring down the reputation of tattooing to the level of the 1920s. The floor was a filthy mess of mud, sawdust, dried spittle, torn newspapers, and wine bottles here and there. The flash on the walls had an even more primitive look than Mephisto's which I had bought from Kellett. The machines were powered by an old direct-current generator which Frank turned on. It made a heluva racket. Randy's needles were as filthy as the ones in Nelson's footlocker, with such a gummy coating of old dried ink-spatters and grease that you were afraid to touch them.

"He's always infectin' someone," Frank said. "How about you? You a clean worker?"

I nodded. "Absolutely antiseptic," I said. "All of this dirty stuff will have to go."

"I'll tell Randy," Frank said. "He can keep his stuff stashed somewhere else while you're around."

I saw that there were going to be great difficulties. "Can't he be antiseptic too?" I asked.

Frank shrugged. "You know how it is," he said. "He's probably too old to change."

"There'll be hell to pay," I said. "And you'll never improve the reputation of the shop as long as he's screwin' up the customers on Monday, Tuesday, Thursday, and Friday, while I'm trying to do good work on Wednesdays and weekends."

Frank shrugged again. "We'll work it out somehow."

And that was that. I moved in on November 11, 1952. Mister Perry was there that day; I had not met him before. He was a small stooped eighty-year old Greek, speaking such badly accented English that he could scarcely be understood. He was about five feet tall, bent almost double and perfectly bald, with twinkling blue eyes. He shaved his head nearly every morning, but sometimes he forgot for a week, and the fine thin strands stood up amusingly. Mr. Perry and I were to get along very well, except for his always insisting that I be there from nine in the morning until closing time at ten p.m., which I could not do. But he was one good friend in a rather terrifying collection of people.

And Randy Webb was there, too, when I moved in. He had to be seen to be believed — a little old man with yellow-brown hair, dressed in stained and spotted pants and a dirty wool shirt, toothless because an irate customer on whom he had put a five-legged panther had knocked his plates out; they broke on the floor and were never replaced. Not only did his chin nearly meet his nose because he lacked teeth, but he had one of the worst complexions imaginable, the result of his wine-drinking. It was covered with rum-blossoms — big scarlet and purple pustules which he was fond of squeezing and popping out about a quarter-teaspoonful of pus and yellow matter. His nose-veins were purple and broken in many places, with resultant spots of purpura; his eyes were red-rimmed and rheumy. Beyond a doubt he was the nastiest-looking person I had yet to see on the street, and the slyest and craftiest back-stabber of all.

He hated me from the beginning, of course. I was the one who threatened his lazy existence and the source of the money for his muscatel. He was penniless most of the time because of his drinking, and he lived in a neighboring flophouse. All of the shop equipment — flash, machines, generator and all, belonged to Mickey Kellett, who by then was taking a cure for alcoholics at a state asylum, having been found one night in a flophouse "lobby" naked, waving a gun, and yelling that the FBI was out to get him and he wouldn't be taken alive.

On that memorable first day when I first went to work down at the shack, I tried to clean up the floor and woodwork somewhat, and laid my nice new machines out in a row. Then I hooked one of them up — and the generator wouldn't work. Randy, in a fit of rage, had completely rewired it so that although the connections looked right, something was wrong. At that time I didn't know enough about electricity and generators to find out what was amiss. Frustrated and furious, I went out and bought three square 6-volt lantern batteries and hooked them to a rheostat, giving myself enough current to work with until I made another arrangement.

Finally Randy came in, smashed as usual. In the two years we worked together I never saw him sober. He stood glowering and weaving just outside the shop, little red eyes meanly glinting. The showdown was at hand. He started to come into the shop, where my needles were laid out on the table.

"Are those my machines?" he said.

"No," I said in a hard and angry tone. "They're mine—and just what the hell have you done to the generator?"

His tone changed. He fawned. "Why, nuthin,' son," he said. "Doesn't it work?"

"You know damned well it doesn't," I said.

"That's a pity," he said, and I caught a faint smile on his drink-raddled face.

A lot of loud and furious talk followed, and then I realized that I was losing by shouting. So I calmed myself and began to use some applied and practical semantics. I told Randy that I was a friend of Mickey Kellett's and had bought the "Mephisto" Nelson stuff from him, and that I was planning to work here and send Mickey some badly needed cash at the Kankakee asylum, so that he could buy cigarettes at the commissary. This confused Randy—for Frank had previously told me that Mickey had let Randy use his equipment if Randy would promise to send him cigarette money—but in eight months Randy had sent nothing. Then—countering with some slyness of my own, I said that since Mr. Perry had hired me, I would have to report what Randy had done to the generator, and Mr. Perry would be angrier than ever, because if I couldn't work I certainly couldn't pay Mr. Perry his thirty-five percent. And so Mr. Perry might have to put Randy out completely, not even leaving him with four days a week. Besides, I added as a finishing touch, with batteries I really didn't need the generator. He missed the gap in my logic at that point.

Randy saw the gates closing, finally and irrevocably. After a few very tense moments he came into the shop and started to re-wire the generator. All this went on with an audience of about a dozen people standing around and saying nothing, somewhat like a mute Greek chorus. After a little work—lo, the generator rattled away once more.

That was only the beginning of the warfare with Randy. He would promise to stop drinking, and then be drunk and stupid within the half-hour. He used tempera colors in the skin—colors which were neither inert nor pure—but very cheap; the tattoos swelled and the color came out. I swore at him, but he went right on with the dangerous pigments. He had a habit, when he was drunk and a customer would rather fearfully inquire about infection, of spitting on the fresh and open tattoo and then rubbing it in, saying "Don't worry about a thing, sonny—you can't infect 'em." He actually believed that the inks themselves were cures for all sorts of diseases from syphilis to skin infections—and this despite the fact that customers were continually returning to him with horrible-looking infected tattoos.

Randy had a pot-bellied crony across the street, a fellow named Jake, who was almost as disreputable and dirty as Randy himself. The kids who got tattoos from him called him "Shaky Jake." Like Randy he was a wino. He had a small shop about four feet wide and nine feet long, an unused corridor in a dry-cleaning shop, as filthy a place as Randy's was before I arrived. Tattooing was only a front for him; he was actually a fence. Just tell Jake what you wanted, and mention the name of the right person who sent you: if he didn't have the item in a room back of the cleaning establishment, he'd send out one of his boys to steal it, and you could have delivery next week. He was fat and always unshaven (I could never discover how he managed always to have a three-day stubble), with dirty grey chest hair about three inches long (his shirt was always open), little pig eyes, and a sour odor from his breath and body. He had a kind of pallid slug-face and teeth that looked like Roquefort cheese. The "roses" that he put on kids looked like four-wheeled propellers on a motor boat. He was perhaps the worst, most careless "artist" on the street. He endangered every tattoo artist by willingly tattooing youngsters from fourteen to seventeen.

After a few weeks it became apparent to Randy that customers were either asking for me to do their work, or waiting until the days when I was on duty. He and Jake devised a scheme to do as much harm as they could to me.

In those days, long before the Stonewall incident, it was imperative that if you were homosexual you had to keep it hidden. Otherwise — if you happened to be a tattoo artist — you would have more tricks than anyone could handle, but you would be bartering blowjobs for tattoos. Randy and Jake decided to spread the word up and down the street — and even told the kids — that I was queer. The word "gay" had not yet ridden like a conquering khan into the language, although in some localities it had made its presence well-known. A rumor like that was hard to kill, but the choicest irony was that they never knew how accurately they had hit the mark. I maintained as cool a front as I could. Once in a while a young man would drop in and look around, and after a time suggest that he would like a free tattoo, in return for which I could enjoy his favors.

"You're barkin' up the wrong tree, buddy," I would say. "Go across the street and ring Shaky Jake's bell. He's the one you want."

After a few weeks of such referrals, both Randy and Jake stopped their talk. And I stopped sending the barter-boys across the street.

One weekend the two old buddies dreamed up a new device to torment me. Both of them knew several corrupt cops, and Jake paid off two of them to look the other way on his business of receiving stolen goods. One of the pair was named Howard. Early on Saturday morning Howard stationed himself outside the arcade in full uniform — and mildly stewed — and told all the entering sailors not to get a tattoo from me, but to go across the street to Jake's. I nearly went wild when one sailor slipped in and told me this. I went outside to confront him and tell him to lay off.

"Sure I will," he said tipsily. "If you'll cut me in after it's all over."

"Yeah," I said, very nervous. "Come back this evening."

Meanwhile Frank, who had an inbuilt anxiety where the fuzz was involved, went to the front of the arcade where the cop could see him, and dialed a number. Then it was the flatfoot's turn to get nervous, for he did not know whether Frank was calling the divisional police commander; after all, he was only a lowly patrolman. He stood first on one foot and then the other, and at last went across the street and disappeared into Jake's cubicle. In a few moments he came out, got into his car and drove away. We saw him no more.

Jake came over the next day with the olive-branch and told me he was sorry, and that if I wanted I could borrow his stencils to copy them. I did not take him up on his offer.

For the next several years Jake and I brushed against each other often. He had a small business going with the removal of tattoos. He would lacerate the surface of the skin with one of his filthy machines, and then apply a paste of silver nitrate or some other keratolytic agent, which usually was unsuccessful. Often the arm got infected, or if it did not, the paste left a puffy dead-white scar the exact outline of the tattoo, having destroyed the melanin layer in the skin. After the initial dislike grew between us, I began to tell customers inquiring about removals to go to a dermatologist, but never to Jake. Our life as neighbors became a kind of uneasy armed truce.

As my business improved, it began to cut into the profits of one tattoo artist up the street, the greatest prima-donna and bullshitter of them all, a guy whose name was Gilbert, but who had adopted the needle-name of "Tatts Thomas." In his opinion there was no other person in the ever-lovin' world who could tattoo at all. He had only scorn for me. "Damned beginners!" he said to a reporter, who hurried right down to my shop to tell me; "they ruin the game for us professionals." I nicknamed him "The Preacher" since he pretended to have such highly moral and ethical ideals about tattooing. He had tattooed through the two World Wars and the Korean and had made quite a lot of money. It was he who was responsible for the Mafia's being interested in tattooing.

Shortly after I opened my shop in 1952, the manager of the arcade where the Preacher worked raised his rent from $90 a month to $200. This would seem to be quite a jump but the figure of $90 was ridiculously low, when you considered that the poorest month for the Preacher still meant a net of a thousand dollars, a figure which doubled during the peak seasonal months of spring and summer. In the 1950s these were handsome amounts. Such easy money enabled the Preacher to drive a luxury car and sport a very large diamond ring. He considered himself the elegant arbiter of the tattoo world.

When the news of his rent raise was given to him, he exploded.

"Goddamn it!" he hollered. "I'll move down on Harrison Street to a shop of my own and I'll take every fuckin' customer away from everybody on the street!"

He reached into his pocket and drew out a thick roll of hundreds. "I could buy and sell every goddamned one of you!" he shouted to the arcade manager.

That was a mistake, for present at that moment was Leo, the manager of another arcade down the street. Leo was front man for the syndicate's Italian or Greek branch—then headed by Louis Arger who owned the arcade. Leo was a very interested listener. It was soon decided by the syndicate to put two tattoo artists in each arcade, and take the market away from the Preacher. The day of the big competition had arrived.

The Preacher, however, was notable for another myth in the tattoo world. He had once read an article somewhere about a European doctor who had tattooed the irises of a blind man to put some color into the dead-white eyeball. The Preacher decided that this was a good foundation on which to try to build some respectability for tattooing—and henceforth he let it be known that the business in his shop was nothing, really; that most of his time was spent in hospital surgeries tattooing eyeballs.

The reporters flocked to him at once, and incautiously—without checking—published all his statements as true. But he made one mistake, telling all of them that he tattooed the "pupils of the eye" instead of irises. Gradually, however, with the advent of colored contact lenses, this little claim to immortality was denied him. A young man once stopped into my shop, and I noticed that he had one blue eye and one brown. Frank and I looked at each other with the same thought: "Let's send him up to the Preacher."

We carefully coached the young man, gave him a few bucks, and sent him on his way.

He came back with a great story. The Preacher, at first unbelievingly, peered into the boy's eyes, and then hemmed and hawed when asked to tattoo one of them so they'd both be the same color. The boy played his part well—how he had read stories in the newspapers about the Preacher's successes, and what admiration he had for the skill required in such an operation. Finally the Preacher in desperation told him he would do it, but the boy had to bring a doctor's authorization, that a great deal of red tape was involved in such an operation, etc., etc., and that really, the difference in the color was not all that noticeable.

The Preacher's array of pretenses did no harm, perhaps, save that they contributed to the inaccurate folklore of tattooing in the American mind.

As the syndicates began to populate their arcades with "jaggers"—by which the permanent tattoo artists meant the incompetent ex-carnival artists, the "deep-working" ones who sent the needles down an eighth of an inch (because you could turn out work more quickly that way), the cut-throat gossip grew worse, and new tricks were invented. If a sailor or a city-boy went into one of the eleven syndicate arcades and asked for Phil Sparrow (a thoughtless and no doubt irritating thing to say to the other "artistes"), the reply was often something like: "Why, *I'm* Phil Sparrow, boy; sit right down and I'll give you one of my famous tattoos," or "Didn't you hear, boy? Very sad. He hung himself last week," or "He's gone out of town," or "He's given up tattooing—he was just an amateur, you know."

Even the Pacific Garden Mission next door got into the act. In those days they had a "Servicemen's Center" which they widely advertised. It was hardly the sort of thing that sailors on their first liberty enjoyed; you could not smoke inside, and the only music allowed was hymns. The swabbies would be given cards as they passed the door and sometimes pulled in bodily for "free food," which consisted of a stale doughnut and a cup of hot brown water they called coffee. Then while the boys were seated, three to each card table, a "missionary" (we said "Mission Mary," although the person was usually male) would come to sit with them to preach to them about God, usually beginning with the question: "Have you accepted Jesus?"

The Mission's religion was the usual holy-roller stuff of the far-right fundamentalist kind, derived from an earlier falwell named Billy Sunday, who had actually been "converted" on their premises. The Mission had fooled the people of Chicago for many years, but few natives—except those who lived on "the street"—knew how they operated. After the doughnuts and coffee and the sermon, the sailors were asked to sign a guest book, giving their mother's name and home address. The unwary young boots always complied. And then about two weeks later, their mothers would get a letter such as this (for I had seen several copies of it which furious boys brought into the shop):

Madame,
We found your son, wandering all alone and lost, in one of the worst Skid Row districts of Chicago; and brought him in and fed him and comforted him, and set his feet on the right path to Great Lakes [or Chanute Field for the airmen; or Fort Sheridan for the soldiers].

Would you not like to contribute something to this worthwhile work? Any contribution you can send us will be gladly received . . .

And the contributions poured in to the tune of about a quarter-million a year, dollar bills and fives, from mothers who envisioned their poor Navy sons far from home, drunk and disorderly in the gutter and rescued from courtmartial or worse by the charitable services of the Pacific [née Beer] Garden [Mission] and its wonderful Christian work of saving souls.

The Mission's "runners," the temporarily reformed drunks who passed out the Mission's cards and scrubbed and swept the premises for five dollars a week, began to expand their efforts. They went up the street to catch the sailors before they reached my shop, telling them not to get a tattoo, they'd regret it, it was sinful to mark their bodies, and all the rest of the dogooder's spiel. As a result I had to hire a lawyer to threaten to report them to the Better Business Bureau for "sharp business practices." The Mission got the word, and stopped their tricks thereafter.

One of the things about the cut-throat life on the "street" was that it left one "unprotected" in a curious sort of way. Academe and the circles I had moved in had sheltered me from contact with raw life. But the "street" reminded me somewhat of Paris where one witnessed a dozen small street dramas every day. Such episodes there were possibly caused by the Frenchman's being half-stewed all day long, and consequently uninhibitedly dramatic. The fact remained that on south State Street in Chicago things happened . . .

. . . like the night, for instance, when a fairly well-dressed wino (at least, with no dried vomit on his shirt) crossed his arms and leaned on Randy's trunk which like Cerberus guarded the entrance to the cubicle. I glanced up briefly — my brush-off glance for non-customers — and returned to reading my paper. But he did not leave, even after a second angrier glance. He looked at me, foolishly vacant, and said "Oh, brother . . ." not the slangy "brother," but more of a compassionate sigh of brotherhood with all mankind . . . "Oh, brother," he said, "this is such a *long* street," and then he turned and went out into the rain again leaving me considerably shattered.

Occasionally there were more drunks on the street than usual. The heart had to be hardened and deadened against them. I started out by giving a quarter to each one who asked for money. But they "put a mark on my gate," so to speak, and on the day when I got thirty-two requests, one after the other, I decided I had to stop. Instead, I would offer them fifty cents to mop or sweep the floor or take out the trash. But the numbers of weak heart, hernia, and sprained back excuses increased so alarmingly fast that I feared for the collective health of the denizens of the neighborhood.

At first I had been fascinated by the mystique of the tattoo world, thinking it filled with friendly persons exchanging information and trade secrets about a harmless hobby. I soon learned better. In the world of business there is little that can compare with the malicious backstabbing, the cut-throat tactics, the trickery and chicanery of the tattoo world. And why should it not be so? A good forty percent of its practitioners in those days was composed of ex-cons or con-men, drunks, wife-beaters, military deserters, pushers, (and even two murderers).

This was the world I had joined. Within six months I had learned more dirty tricks than I had ever known previously. It was necessary for survival. There was a bulldog in me which kept me from retreating again into the world I had left — although the memory of the dullness and peace of Academia (even with its intramural wars) proved very attractive in those moments when I was not thinking of money. "Peace after warre / Port after stormie seas . . . doth greatly please," as Spenser said. But he was a court poet and had never enjoyed the diet of mixed greens—fives, tens, and twenties—that we did on the street.

*   *   *   *   *

The mutual back-stabbing scenes that went on between Randy and myself grew more and more violent. Randy devised one that really backfired on him. He told another alcoholic cop on the beat, whom he probably paid off, that I was tattooing boys under eighteen, and to come in to give me a hard time. And John did—standing flatfootedly with his purple nose at the entrance to the tattoo shack and making accusations until I began to suspect why, and asked him directly. His actions and attitude confirmed the suspicion. I called Frank from the rear of the arcade and the three of us had a chat. Sometime during the encounter I pulled a ten-dollar bill from my pocket and gave it to John.

"If Randy gave you five, here's ten," I said. "Be on my side after this."

"Yeah," Frank added, "it's really Randy who's tattooing the kids."

After the cop left, I had an idea. On the street there was no worse crime than to be an informer. That was exactly what Randy (and I, of course) had done—finked to the cops. Thereafter I began to tell the story of Randy's transferring himself to the side of the law—choosing a few gabby souls as auditors. I could almost hear a triumphant flourish of trumpets the day Randy apologized for the whole episode, and asked me to stop spreading my story around.

"Nobody'll talk to me in the bars any more," he whined. "They all think I'm a fink."

"Okay," I said, "if you'll stop spreading the rumor that I'm queer."

But the last and major confrontation was soon to arrive. Mickey Kellett showed up one day, released from the alcoholic ward at Kankakee state hospital. Randy at once disappeared with him to celebrate. The next day Mickey came into the arcade, his face the color of tallow, beard mark showing blue, a patch on his forehead where he had "slipped on the ice" and fallen down. His hands were a curious shiny brown-purple color, as if he had some circulation impairment. I could feel something in the air. Randy was limping, his leg and ankle swollen from drinking. The two old cronies had their heads together, whispering.

The next day when I went to work I discovered what it was all about. Mickey Kellett had installed himself in the shop and put all my machines in a pile. He announced firmly that he was going to take back his shop. He stood glowering under his green eye-shade behind the fastened baby-gate, and told me to stay out.

"You can have the place on Mondays, if you want. But that's all. Randy and I will run it the rest of the time."

Mr. Perry was in the hospital having a colostomy tube inserted in his side. Frank and I went to see him. The poor old Greek wailed with happiness to see us. When we told him what had happened, he told me to go back and tell both Randy and Mickey to get out, that the shop was mine, and he didn't want to see either of them again. When we left I asked Frank to carry the news to them, and said I would be down the next day after they had left.

Everything was gone — even the nails and screws in the wall had been pulled out, all electrical wiring removed — everything except the pink linoleum baseboard I had put up and the black paint I had applied. There was nothing left except the ceiling and the three empty walls of the shack.

Sighing, I set to work. I had been making my own flash during the weeks that Randy and I had been working together. All that remained was to hang it up and set up my own equipment. The generator was gone. I used storage batteries and a charger. I had to install new wiring and a cabinet to hold stencils, but in two days I was ready.

Meanwhile word reached me that Randy had laughed and said "Phil won't last two weeks there if I move out." He and Mickey decided to open their own shop — two rooms in the Fleetwood flop-house next door. They had some cards printed: "40 years Experience. 10,000 designs: American, European, Oriental." They tripled the prices on all designs, a sure way to lose customers. Within a week I saw two pieces of Mickey's tattooing. I had believed Randy to be the worst tattooist in the United States, but Mickey won out.

In three weeks their shop was closed, and the Fleetwood was holding all their equipment for non-payment of their $10 a week rent. They had drunk up all their profits, and no more customers came.

A great calm descended. I resigned from the university on the day that a week's net from tattooing equaled a month's salary from teaching. But in the autumn one of the temporary workers in the arcade, whom Frank had fired for stealing money from the peepshow machines, went to the police. They fell upon the place, found Frank's dirty machines and eight-pager books, and closed everything. I found a new location across the street and moved in. Thus after two years I finally had a place of my own and was independent.

The feeling was wonderful — no more fat little university deans giving orders, no papers to grade, no responsibilities except to pay my rent and enjoy myself. I figuratively flushed my PhD diploma down the drain and started a new life.

PART III

Doctor Kinsey [Prometheus] and the Shop

Good fortune led me to become acquainted with Dr. Kinsey in the late 1940s. A friend introduced me to him and I went through one of his statistical interviews on my sexuality. This was the beginning of a long and very close friendship which lasted until his death in 1956. I became one of his unofficial "collaborators" with the Institute for Sex Research at Indiana University in Bloomington. We helped the work of the Institute by steering it towards interesting people or things, or guiding *them* towards it.

Dr. Kinsey was one of the warmest personalities I had ever met. He was then in his fifties, a cordial gregarious man as approachable as an old park bench, and just as much of an accomplished con-man as I was later to become in my tattoo career. He deliberately cultivated the "con" approach so that he could win the trust of the person being interviewed. In like manner he took up smoking and drinking (very, very gingerly) to put his interviewees at ease. His warmth and approachability were further enhanced by his talent for talking to the most uneducated hustlers and prostitutes and pimps in their own language, no matter how coarse. It gained trust for him among the suspicious ones, and word of his honesty and discretion opened doors for him that would have remained forever closed to a more academic attitude. If in his later days he changed a little under "the weight of being great," to use Gertrude Stein's phrase, it did not alter the essential inquisitiveness and curiosity of the man; "curiosity" is used in its best and deepest sense, for more than any other person I knew he wanted to find out what went on inside people, what made them tick. The Latin motto, *Nothing that is human is strange to me*, might very well have been his own.

He knew that my discontent with the academic matrix was increasing, and when he finally learned of my decision to remove myself as far as possible from the ivied nursery, he reacted with perhaps the only critical statement I had ever heard him make: "Oh my God, no," he said. "I have never interviewed anyone who didn't say he wanted his tattoo off." Years later Dr. C.A. Tripp consoled me by saying that most psychiatrists and priests are notoriously shockable, a reaction often seen in the "moralism" of many of them.

Considering Kinsey's general unshockability in almost everything, his forthright disapproval somewhat nettled me. Even though it was winter and not a good time to find tattoos exposed on arms and chests, I began my own investigation on the arms of counter-clerks in drug-stores, lunch-counters, and elsewhere. The reactions of those queried were largely favorable. One boy said, "Chee, no—I like mine. I wouldn't take anything for it," proudly displaying a rather poorly done eagle. Another said, "It reminds me of my days in the Navy. I like it."

Out of about fifty persons only about five regretted having their skin marked. When this was reported to Kinsey he shrugged, grinned, and said, "Well, perhaps your method of approach is better than mine," and then went on to a further analysis: "Of course. They are not trying to put themselves on their best behavior with you. There's no sense of guilt when you ask them."

After a month or two had passed in my new career, his scientific curiosity began to assert itself. One evening over dinner he said, "We really ought to take advantage of you."

"How so more than you already have?" I asked, sardonic.

"You are probably one of a half dozen literate tattoo artists in the country—if indeed that many. And we've noticed tattoos on hundreds of persons during our interviews. But they seem totally unable to tell us why they got them, and we don't have the time to probe as deeply as we would like into that aspect."

"So . . .?" I said.

"Keep a journal for us on what you can perceive as the sexual motivations for getting tattooed. You may not be a trained scientific observer, but you have a writer's keen eye, and you should be able to unearth a great deal.''

And so I began a journal for him which was kept faithfully until even two years after his death. As it progressed he grew more and more fascinated with the sexual implications of tattooing, and flattered me by saying that he found information in it which he was certain had never appeared in print before, suggesting that eventually we might collaborate on a monograph about it, but his untimely death in 1956 ended that project. But he decided, during his interviewing of the inmates at San Quentin, that a question about tattooing might be added to the general questionnaire. This was done, but the findings were slight, since he later told me that most of the prisoners with tattoos were not able to analyze nor even express their reasons for wanting or getting one.

On several occasions Kinsey visited my shop, more or less incognito, spending five or six hours there on a busy Saturday. He talked to the sailors and others, asking loaded questions that seemed entirely innocent. At the end of one such session, when we had both learned much from his skillful probing, he said, ''I think that every social worker or psychologist should be compelled to spend at least five full days in field work in a tattoo shop before he gets his degree.''

He made his first visit while my shop was still in the old arcade. As luck would have it, Randy was there, and for a wonder fairly sober. When I introduced the two, Randy's mouth fell open on his raw red maw and his eyes popped open wide. ''Not THE Doctor Kinsey?'' he said.

Kinsey grinned. ''The same,'' he said.

''Well, I'll be damned,'' Randy said. And then they fell to talking, with Randy pulling out all the old folklore stories about tattooing.

I finally said, ''Randy, Doctor Kinsey is here as a scientist. Cut the bullshit and tell him the real story.''

Randy looked sheepish. ''Guess you're right, Phil,'' he said, and after that the talk was more realistic. Kinsey asked him questions about the percentage of sexual action tattoos, of which there was very little indeed. Randy exposed all his tattoos and with urging even gave his memorized and poorly pronounced "carnival spiel" while he was the "Tattooed Man" with circuses and county fairs. He even exposed the small faded butterfly which had been tattooed on his penis thirty years before. Kinsey said that this was the first tattoo in such a place that he had seen.

"Why did you get it on your cock?" he asked.

Randy laughed. "Mostly as a gag," he said, "because everyone seems to be real interested in that kind of a tattoo. And partly for business reasons. They're sure to remember you and your name if you've got a tattooed dong. Then they tell others and you get more business."

In my journal everything was included which I thought might be of interest or significance to Kinsey. After my own shop was opened across the street we even for a time discussed the idea of a tape-recorder close to the scene of operation. But nothing came of that largely because of the endless repetitions that he would hear, and also because of the difficulty of knowing just when to turn on the recorder to get the really important information. Instead, the material was recorded as faithfully as possible in the journal. Since he was mainly interested in the sexual motivations of tattooing, my questions to clients were formed to lead in that direction whenever possible.

Some interesting segments of information related to just what the guys did after they got their tattoos. If the situation was right and the mood relaxed enough, a returning customer would be asked what he had done on the evening after he got his first tattoo. Four questions were asked as casually as possible.

"Well," I might say, after some initial badinage, "how did your tattoo turn out?"

"Fine," he might reply, "but it itched—" or "everybody kept hitting me on it . . ."

"People generally do one of four things after a first tattoo," I would say. "They either get drunk or get in a fight, or get a piece of ass, or go home and stand in front of a mirror and jack off. What did you do?"

It is not a statistically significant sampling, but out of hundreds of "returnees" these were the results. Many of them, of course, simply laughed and made no reply.

1. The boys who came back and said — either with questioning or without — that after their tattoo they went out and fucked a girl 1724
2. Boys who got into a fight following a tattoo 635
3. Boys who said that all they did was get drunk afterwards (over 800 of question #1 also said this) 231
4. Number admitting they masturbated while admiring their new tattoo 879

Each response was interesting, and each in a way reflected the feeling of manliness that accompanies the new tattoo. There was no way of knowing how many of them answered truthfully or how many were merely bragging. But it would not be surprising to learn that those who did answer were really telling the truth.

Such a conclusion is based on one of the most astonishing discoveries I made early on about what might be called the mystique of the tattoo: a kind of temporary love affair between artist and customer. If conditions are precisely right, and no one else in the shop, the customer's defenses fall as soon as the needle starts its work; and he tells the artist things which (I feel sure) he has never told his wife or his girl-friend or his best buddy. The tattoo artist becomes for him a psychiatrist, priest, best boyfriend, mother, father — a kind of "blood confessor," and for a little while one can almost notice a lingering incense as the dingy shop becomes a sort of shadowed confessional. An explanation for this mystique was never forthcoming, although much was surmised — thinking that perhaps the fact that the tattooist for a brief moment held absolute power over the person — was a power-figure, almost like a god — and could therefore be absolutely trusted, and if that were so, would then never reveal the most intimate confidences. It remained to the end of my tattoo experience the most fascinating question to ponder, and continues to hold me captive to the present.

Kinsey was particularly interested in a letter which I received very early in the tattoo experience, which is here quoted in part:

Dear Phil,

I stood and watched you for a long time the other night. You had a lot of sailors in the shop. I think that you must have the most romantic occupation in the world. I have always liked sailors. You come closer to them than anybody. Does it not give you a feeling of domination over them to tattoo them? Do you not feel that the Sailor thereafter carries around with Him, to the end of His days, your mark upon Him? And does not the act of tattooing become the testing of Him? If He flinches, are you not His Master? Is He not the slave, bearing your mark?

Or from another angle, does not the Sailor thereafter carry with Him your own creation beneath His skin? Do you not symbolically go with Him to the far places?, the far suns and seas, the bamboo huts of savages and the stone lacework of Indian castles, the crystal pools and sands of Persia, white columns against the dark blue Greek skies, the golden suns and fountains of red-walled Rome? Do you not with Him hear mermaids singing? Can you not know a little, then, of a way of life which is denied to most of us? Do you not (a small part of you in Him, in His skin) actually accompany the Sailor on His far wanderings? Are you not part of Him, flesh of His flesh? When, panting and naked, He braces Himself on His strong bronzed young thighs to guide Himself between her legs, do you not ride high on His shoulder in the design you applied there? Or are you not crushed between His brave and swelling pectorals and her flattened breast? Or ride the bucking-horse from the peak-point of His pelvic bone? You are with the Sailor forevermore . . .

And did He not receive you with His blood? Are you not — and your skill — coupled with Him in a mystic vow of comradeship? Is it not a kind of Romany gesture, a gypsy blood-brother oath that you have taken with him? You, the sadist, have drawn His blood, you have injected your fluid . . .

and so on for another page. It was from a man, using an obvious pen-name. Turgid and over-written though the prose is, it nonetheless reveals much about the observer's reaction to tattooing, and underlines the mystique of the act. Kinsey was particularly interested in the obvious masochism of the writer as well as the capitalization of all words relating to the sailor, an obvious deification of a sexual object.

There is no denying the high sexual significance of tattooing for many people. One cold snowy evening a sailor came into my shop all alone and got his first tattoo: an anchor on his forearm. After it was finished and bandaged, he asked if there were a head in the place. I told him where the toilet was, and he went back to it.

He was gone a little too long to urinate and not long enough for something more weighty. Moreover, when he came back, waved goodbye and left, I was struck by one curious thing: I had not heard the toilet flush.

I went back to investigate. The sailor had masturbated and spread the still-steaming ejaculate all over the cold cement floor. Kinsey was quite interested in this confirmation of our jointly-developed theories about tattoos and the assertion of masculine status, narcissism, and the sexual aftermath of a first tattoo. "Graphic proof," he said. "And it happened right under your nose."

"Well . . . not exactly," I said.

When Kinsey was observing in the shop I always used my best lines of patter to steer the customers into his areas of interest. This was not hard to do, since hope springs eternal in the human genitalia, especially those of sailors. With his fresh scientific eye he saw and commented on things which—because I had seen them so often—I had not taken the trouble to record in my journal. But after he noticed and commented later about their nervous fingering of their genitals, and the half-tumescence that some of them showed, I remembered that I had noted such things so often that they had slipped into unawareness.

Kinsey's presence in the shop was always a stimulus, and the afternoons and evenings he spent there assured everyone pleasure and excitement. Early in our association I began to call him Doctor Prometheus, fire-(and light) bringer to mankind. His early death, brought on by his unceasing overwork, his many trips to California to interview sexual offenders in prison, was much regretted. But had he rested instead, or controlled the demon within, he would not have been Doctor Kinsey.

If one really believed in an afterlife it would be pleasant to consider Kinsey sitting with Socrates and Plato under the shade of an ilex tree, and discussing the *Phaedrus*, or asking Leonardo da Vinci about his golden youths, or Michelangelo about the models he used, or Whitman to tell the real truth about himself and Peter Doyle. Questioning and questing, he would have all eternity to roam in — and if he ever came to the end, he would still be unsatisfied.

PART IV

Sex and the Tattoo: Motivations

A new sign on the wall of the new shop drew a lot of comment. It read: "Depressed? Downhearted? A good tattoo may make you feel like a man again." It needed no more confirmation of its basic truth than the casual comment of one sailor after he had an anchor put on. He looked down at it and said, "Y'know, it makes me feel just a little bigger with that tattoo a-sittin' there on my arm."

Something was slowly going wrong with the young American male, it seemed to me. His concept of the Hero had been removed and he was searching to find it again.

The destruction of the Hero had begun long before the advance of equal rights for women and the gradual shift of the country to the permissiveness of a matriarchy in the 1960s. This particular thesis had been bitterly stated in the 1920s when Philip Wylie wrote *Generation of Vipers* and invented the term and concept of "Momism." The female was appropriating what had up to then been the exclusive property of the male.

And the search for the Hero went on in another direction, seeking him in the role of Breadwinner, where the rights of the male were again being challenged—not only by the rivalry of women in the workplace, but by the growth of automation. The computers and machines of the 1950s were slowly replacing the male's skills and services.

Finally, the concept of the Hero as Warrior had been destroyed. Man with his bow and arrows, his shotguns and rifles, had been made impotent by the development of nuclear fusion and fission— for what Warrior was brave enough to fight the little killing sun of Hiroshima? And what could he do if he were?

Perhaps, then, on the basis of an obscure feeling about the decline of his role as Hero, a dwindling of his importance, one could erect a number of motives for getting tattooed—along with thousands of other rationales pointing towards a renewal of self-esteem. In the shadowed murky brain of the average customer in my shop no analysis could take place. To a direct question about why he was getting tattooed he could only say "Chee, I dunno," or "I guess I just like 'em, that's all." I realized quite early that if I were going to be of any assistance to Kinsey I would have to develop and use roundabout methods to get any answers.

Gradually it began to be clear that there were indeed many motivations for getting tattooed. Some were more common than others, and perhaps in a majority of cases there was an overlapping or merging between categories. Some of the motives might appear— and did—in thousands of examples; others in only two or three. Most of the motives were sexual; several were "pure"—that is, not noticeably overlapping or even connected with sexuality. Some were "mixed"—pure in certain cases, and sexual in others; and a final grouping was questionably pure.

The observations together with illustrative examples are tentatively presented here—not as final and definitive conclusions but more in the nature of provocative departure points for further investigations.

DECORATION

Decoration is a questionably "pure" motive, in certain instances decidedly sexual with the purpose of attracting the opposite sex—or perhaps even the same sex. It is a very small category, but it includes the sailor who blurted out enthusiastically when he saw the finished work: "Jesus! I think that's the purtiest thing I ever saw! I'd rather wear that than a new suit!" as well as the slow words of the physician-husband of an elderly woman who was almost completely covered with tattoos: "I really believe that—to me at least— they are more beautiful for her to wear than diamonds."

HERD INSTINCT

"All the guys in my gang has got 'em, and I want one," said the youngest member of a Chicago gang called the "Road Wolves." This motive overlaps with one that might be called "Tradition," in which all sailors might be included. For a very large percentage of the young "boots" who came into my shop from the Great Lakes Naval Training Station about forty miles north of Chicago, a tattoo officially changed the "boot" from a civilian to an old salt. It allied him with all the old sea-dogs he had ever heard of, and was a badge that for a few years he wore with pride.

To be included also in the very large numbers of this category would be those who wanted "to keep up with the Joneses," particularly when this motive applied to the younger crowd, whether a gang member or merely a schoolmate or the boy down the block. If one got a tattoo, all his friends wanted one as well.

NARCISSISM

There are two types here: a true and a false. The genuine narcissist would no more think of adorning or decorating his body than he would of going to bed with a wooden Indian. His body is perfect as it is; he is delighted with it. But the pseudo-narcissist believes that if he already has a good body he can further beautify it with tattoos. Should he later turn into the true type, he will be very unhappy to discover that his tattoos now mar his "beauty" — and incidentally, make his winning of any Mr. Universe contest an impossibility. Such was the case of Axel, a weightlifter, who would have given anything to have his innumerable torso-tattoos removed.

EXHIBITIONISM

It was always amazing to realize how many persons wanted to show off their tattoos. If I asked a prospective customer whether he were already tattooed, he would rarely answer with a simple "yes." Instead, he would whip off his jacket and shirt or roll up his sleeve to show me what he already had. One homosexual hanger-on

in the shop, a taxi-driver named Francis, was more than delighted to
show his tattooed genitals to anyone who happened to be in the
shop, particularly if it were a handsome young man. I finally had to
tell him to stop. Francis later had a complete mental breakdown;
part of his cure was that his psychiatrist forbade him ever to enter a
tattoo shop again.

I had often wondered why so many young men got tattooed on
the left biceps instead of the right one. Only after a number of years
did I hear one of them declare that if he had it on the left, he could
hang that arm out of the car window while driving, and show it to
the girls—a motive with an overlap into that of "sexual attractiveness."

A darkly handsome young Italian once dropped in for no other
reason than to tell me he had tattooing all over his genitals.

"So?" I said, not inviting him to show them to me.

"Yeah," he said. "I done it all in jail." Wherewith he whipped
out his penis. It was literally black with very crude self-applied
writing. There was a small black cherry surrounded by the usual
wording of "Here's mine—Where's yours?" There were also the
words: "God's gift to women," as well as "Let me slide this long
stiff pole into you."

"Well," I said, searching for a comment. "There's not room for
much more."

He was insulted because he thought that my words belittled the
size of his dingdong, and he left.

Time after time old winos—and many other types—came into
my shop to show me their ancient faded tattoos, put on by Charlie
Wagner or Bert Grimm or some other near-legendary figure. Eventually it became rather boring.

POSSESSION

Here again is a double category. On one side is the pride that
many persons took in the simple act of owning a tattoo: "It's mine;
no one can take it away from me."

This is a fairly "pure" motivation, but the other side of it is
sexually complicated. Earl, a youthful gang member in Chicago,
heavily tattooed, and looking fierce as a young Valentino with side-

burns down to his jawline, one evening brought in his young wife and demanded that his name be put high on her leg. She was too embarrassed to lower her levis while I was present so I stepped outside. When I went back she had put on Earl's shirt and sat with her fat white thighs pressed close together. She yelled and squirmed a lot while I put on a small rose with Earl's name beneath.

When it was done she stood up and Earl suddenly grabbed her from behind, naked lust in his eyes and gestures. If they had been alone he would have topped her there and then. You could almost see his mind working: "She's my woman, I made her get tattooed, and now that she *is* mine, I want her." The tension of his face, the intensity of his eyes, the muscular contractions of his arms and torso as he grabbed her should have been camera-recorded for posterity, stag films, and Doctor Kinsey.

A heavily tattooed young Sicilian brought in his waitress girl-friend; each had a small heart bearing the other's initials put over the left nipple. Another man wanted some writing on his arm obliterated; it stated that Nick was Sue's forever — and he no longer was. Still another young man was rejected by his girl because he had a previous girl-friend's name on his arm. During the eighteen years that I tattooed, I covered literally thousands of such reminders of early romance.

A husband came in with his wife and wanted tattooed on one of her breasts the words "I belong—" and on the other "to Johnny." When it was finished he handled her almost as excitedly as had Earl, and said "Now, by God, you're my woman!" The feeling of complete possession was undoubtedly mixed with the complete submission of the woman to the man's dominance. Over the years nearly a hundred men brought in their women to have the man's name inscribed above the celestial gate, or on the gluteus maximus. After I had moved to California and been discovered by the Hells Angels, I marked their women's breasts many times with "Property of—" followed by the member's gang-name.

This category also includes the thousands of young men who had their girls' names inscribed in hearts or roses on their arms. Within six months many of the young men were back to have the name blacked-out or flowered-in. Often I tried to talk them out of having a name put on, saying that "there's many a slip between the tattoo needle and the wedding-bed," but most of them—with the positiveness of the young—always knew that the situation which existed at the moment was sure to last forever. Often I asked if they were married to the girl; if they were not, I advised against the name. But of course they knew better.

SADOMASOCHISM

Occasionally there were instances of simple masochism, like the men who asked me now and then for a "dry run"—trace a design or merely scribble with a needle having no pigment in it, so that they "could see how it feels." I certainly lacked sophistication the first time a person asked me for a dry run. But when he suddenly tensed, gasped, and his mouth took on the characteristic fish-mouth shape of orgasm, my ignorance was quickly erased. Thereafter all requests for a dry-run were met with my best blank stare. "I don't understand," I would say. "I'm here to put designs on the skin, not to play games. I can show you what it feels like—" and here demonstrated how an absolutely perpendicular application of the needle to the tip of the thumb gave the sensation of a tattoo but did not break the skin. Such an offer never seemed to satisfy the dry-run kids, however.

One afternoon an ugly heavyset little man about forty years old came into the shop and looked around; and after a bit of uncertainty asked me if I would "tattoo any place." Such a request always referred to the genital region. I told him there was a minimum price for such jobs.

"Well, I have a lot of work on me down here," he said and made a vague hand movement around his crotch, "and would like to have some more."

He stepped behind the screen and lowered his trousers. His whole groin and the regions on each side of his genitals as well as the lower inner thighs were covered with tattoos—busts of big breasted women all looking towards the center. His penis was covered with over thirty small tattoos—stars, flowers, symbols—and along the top of it lay a poorly executed naked girl.

"I have one little space right here," he said, showing me the underside of the glans at the corona edge near the frenum, "where I'd like to have a small flower."

"That's quite a lot of work you have," I said with a neutral inflection.

"Yeah," he said. "Sure proves I ain't queer, huh? All them gurls . . ."

"Oh sure," I said.

"Lots of fun when you go to the whorehouse," he said. "All the gurls can't get over it. They'll lay it in their hand and holler, 'Oh, Flo—c'mere; I wanna show you sumpin.'"

"A lot of fun," I said.

I got out the slanted bench and laid him on it, and started to apply the small flower. Tattooing a penis is extremely difficult. Since the skin has to be taut to get the color in—and since the penis is usually flaccid from subconscious fear, and because it seems to have a life of its own—trying to get back into the belly or wriggle from side to side when the needle approaches—I was not paying much attention to the state of tumescence,.except that I noted its growing rigidity. All of a sudden he gasped and ejaculated.

It startled me. I threw some tissues at him. "Gee, Phil," he said. "Guess the ole imagination was jes' workin' overtime."

"Well," I said, "you might as well relax and enjoy it."

After the orgasm, he was no longer interested in having the flower finished, but I went on anyway. It was very painful for him after the ejaculation; he was suffering a great deal. And his embarrassment was total; he mumbled a goodbye as soon as possible after paying me, and I never saw him again.

Many times genuine masochists came for tattoos; perhaps one should say "extreme" instead of "genuine." A man about forty-five—tall and bald and very nervous—asked to speak to me in the back room. There he showed me his chest on which were a half-dozen old tattoos including one of a nude girl standing upright. He wanted all of them covered. The genital region of the girl figure had been deeply burned out with a cigarette. His nipples were a disaster: one of them had been torn or bitten off completely, and the other was dangling by a thin filament of flesh.

I told him that the designs were too old and too black to be covered, and suggested that what was needed here was reconstructive plastic surgery and not more tattooing.

Most of the masochists who came to see me were homosexual, although there were some definitely heterosexual ones; one husband even brought his wife especially so that she could watch while he suffered. With him — as with so many of the customers — there were definite signs of sexual arousal. The reasons for these reactions will be left to novelists and psychiatrists.

RIVALRY

Rivalry, or keeping up with the Joneses, is a small category but a fairly important one. It stems from the red-blooded American's desire to have just as good a car as his neighbor's, as many TV sets, telephones, refrigerators and stereos. Often when a crowd of four or five young men entered, one would say to another: "I've just *gotta* get another one. I got five now, but Jim's got six." Or: "He ain't gonna get ahead of me — slap it on. I'll keep up with him if it's the last thing I ever do."

Such guys could not stand the idea of their buddies getting ahead of them. The quality of the tattoo — or the choice of design — seemed not to matter. I had one boy once who got seventeen stars put on his arm in a cluster, simply to surpass his friend who had twenty tattoos. Naturally, every small star — made with a single continual movement of the needle as they used to be made with a pencil in grade school — counted as another tattoo for him.

HOMOSEXUALITY

Homosexuality is an interesting grouping among these motivations. When I started tattooing and keeping the journal for Kinsey, I also began to keep a record of the number of tattoos and their descriptions and prices, for tax purposes. In the years of tattooing in Chicago and later in California, I put on well over a hundred thousand tattoos, covering quite a few acres of skin. Of that number it seemed to me that fewer than one percent were put on *obvious* homosexuals — those who could be recognized either by their actions or by what they said to friends who came in with them — or by the tingle in my left elbow. But this was all long before the leather movement or the Stonewall liberation incident—and these remarks would not of course hold true for the present time; today's openness would perhaps change much.

The reason for the reluctance of homosexuals to get tattooed in those days was not far to seek. One of the important bases of the syndrome is vanity, and if that is true it is easily admitted that many homosexuals did not want to spoil their bodies with anything so vulgar as a tattoo. Kinsey agreed with this explanation, although he carefully pointed out to me that homosexuality had many complicating factors in addition to narcissism. Not that I was unaware of that fact—but like any good scientist he was taking nothing for granted. Some kind of nut once suggested that perhaps the general impermanence of homosexual relationships disposed them not to have any permanent decorations; we will leave that point for discussion at the monthly group therapy session.

One change, however, came about in the homosexual attitude towards tattoos around 1954 following the national release of the movie *The Wild One* with Marlon Brando; the original motorcycle film, it seemed to crystallize or release, the obscure and long-hidden feelings of many homosexuals. In a sense the so-called leather movement began with this movie, and the pounding hearts of many persons sitting in darkened theatres told them that here was something they had been wanting for a long time. Suddenly through the dim and obscure shadowings surrounding the Death and Disappearance of the Hero there began to be seen the vague outlines of a new and exciting replacement. Kinsey added the term "s/m" to his "little language," the one used by him and his colleagues so that they might discuss openly at restaurants some of the details that might have called in the falwell squads had they been completely understood—H for homosexual, HT for heterosexual, TV for transvestite, A/G for anal-genital, and so forth.

In the tattoo shop there began to appear motorcyclists in leather—leather everywhere, jackets, pants, jockstraps, caps, boots and belts—and keys right and left, chains and silver studs. Often it seemed overdone: one elegant in full leather had three inches of black leather filigree lacework sewed to the bottom of his leather pants to lengthen them.

These leather guys began to get symbolically violent tattoos—black panthers crawling up the arms, or daggers or snakes or skulls or combinations of all the symbols of death and violence and sexuality and masculinity. I was overwhelmed by the sudden appearance of so many of these figures, and abandoned all records as the impulse of many homosexuals to be considered more masculine—by the addition of a tattoo—grew stronger.

Even before this leather movement began, however, there were undoubtedly many homosexuals getting tattooed or at least coming into the shop—perhaps as many as twenty percent of the visitors were homosexuals whom I was unable to recognize as such. Typical example: a sailor named Ed fooled me for many years. He got his first tattoo as a boot from Great Lakes, returned several times for other designs, and finally disappeared for four years. When he returned he came with his sailor buddy—and this time got a rose with a double banner carrying his name and that of Chuck, his buddy. Ed was very proud of the decor he had got on his genitals in the Orient—a small "6" and a "9" on each underside of the glans, separated by the frenum; a small delicate yellow octopus on the dorsal side of the shaft; a little ring around the base of the shaft with a small red heart set as the stone—"so's I'll always have a heart-on," he giggled.

The clientele in the shop—mainly sailors and young members of street gangs, and in general males between eighteen and twenty-five—made my place a great hunting ground for cruising homosexuals. Often, though it was rather painful for me to do it, I had to ask the "hunter" to leave. If I had permitted a free and open meat-rack atmosphere, the shop would have been well-filled all of the time—but I would have had no business at all. Despite the vigilance that had to be exercised to protect my business, it was obvious to me that many assignations were made behind my back. A one-man operation is a difficult thing to handle, especially if you have twenty or thirty persons in the shop at one time, running into the backroom to the toilet.

Occasionally an older homosexual would bring his young hustler friend in for a tattoo. One such pair was typical—an aging Ivy-Leaguer named Jack, and his handsome tough-looking ex-boxer friend named Rich, who looked Italian but turned out to be Polish and German. Rich wanted a king cobra high on his shoulder; he had a couple of other tattoos which he had got in the Philippines during his Navy experience. Jack hovered over him like a mother-hen while the work was being done, and even asked if I had to hold Rich's shoulder so tightly! His eye was jealous, and his attitude a mixture of wife, father, brother, and lover. Rich was very proud of his "built," and got a good deal of work from me, his mentor always trying to get me to reduce my prices. Rich later—after they broke up—continued to have more work done, and proved to be generous as well as good-looking.

Another aging guy brought in a young hustler named Terry, who was evidently taking his keeper for a great deal of money. Terry already had some crudely done "pokey" tattoos, put on in jail, as well as a pachuco cross on his left hand between thumb and forefinger, and a gang-recognition dot on his cheek. He wanted the pachuco cross covered, and a message put on his right shoulder-blade. The inscription was: "Till the end, Russ," with the date beneath it: February 16, 1958. After that, he talked Russ into getting one, and the older man—protesting loudly that it was his first and last—with many squirmings and ladylike little shrieks had me write: "Love, Terry," and the same date.

As they were about to leave Terry said, "Well, I may see you again."

"Not I!" said Russ.

"Not even to get it covered up?" I asked Russ slyly.

But if either of them got the writing covered, it was done in some other shop.

A rather interesting "mixed" case once came to my attention. A boy came in with a rose tattoo on his arm, and the name "Mike" in the banner beneath it. He wanted "Mike" covered with small flowers.

As I started to do it, I idly asked, "Are you thinking of going incognito through the rest of your life?"

"Oh, that's not *my* name," he said. "I used to be gay but I gave all that up when I accepted Jesus a year ago."

"No more problems with being gay then?" I said.

"No indeed," he said firmly. "I never think of men now."

He paused a moment. "Except when I jack off," he said.

It was Pope, I think, who pointed out the connection between bliss and ignorance, and the folly of being wise.

And finally, a young homosexual just turned eighteen brought in a curious design to be put on his arm. It was an outline drawing of two men's heads in a kissing position, but their profiles had melted into each other, so that the nose of each was in the center of the other's head. At first I objected to putting it on him, saying that such a design obviously branded him and advertised his homosex.

"What would your mother say?" I asked. "She would only have to look at this to know you're gay."

"Oh, she doesn't mind," he said. "Anyways, she says that my goin' out with boys saves her a lot of money, and is a lot cheaper than givin' me the money to take girls out."

CRYPTO-HOMOSEXUALITY

The ratio of homosexual and heterosexual which exists in every man and woman, and which Kinsey attempted to measure with his rating scale of zero to six, was never easily detected in connection with motivations for tattoos. Now and then you could see small signs of it: a sailor would come in and say he wanted a tattoo "just like his buddy's," or one that he had seen on an old salt at Great Lakes Training Station. Or a young man might say that he wanted a black panther or other design "because my uncle had one like it." Just how much connection there is between latent homosexuality and what is called male-bonding is a question one might well ask Ernest Hemingway to explain, and he died from a shotgun blast in his mouth after having written about male friendships all his life. Some degree of sublimation must have taken place in many such mixed personalities, for on the surface most of them seemed to be heterosexually oriented. But it was sometimes amusing to see a young boot sailor's friend come in with him for moral support and then notice that during the most painful part of the procedure, the customer was tightly clutching his buddy's hand, who usually held it in both of his own for added reassurance.

When a younger fellow got tattooed, and had brought with him an older friend, the relationship between them was often a prime example of male-bonding. The older one, standing in a frankly heroic light to the younger, embodied the same kind of mentorship that I had seen many times before. Should the younger one turn woozy, the older would go for a glass of water and hover over him with worried eyes. The younger would try to hide his embarrassment in a hastily summoned show of bravado, or attempt to rationalize his defection from the macho by saying something like "I ain't had nuttin' to eat since breakfast."

MANHOOD INITIATION RITE

Many times young men getting a first tattoo asked if the skin could be deadened beforehand, to which they got a joking reply that this was a man's mark they were getting, and they would just have to stand the pain.

In our society today there is no real ceremonial to mark the passing from puberty to manhood. Early in the 1900s boys wore short pants, and their graduation to long ones was a ritual symbol of their achievement of adulthood. By mid-century knickers were rarely seen, not even on the golf course, and even the merest toddlers were wearing long trousers. Within the confines of the Catholic religion confirmation was still practiced, but was a fairly meaningless gesture in society as a whole.

A tattoo marked the arrival of adulthood for many young men. None of them was aware that the roots of such an association might have reached very far back, to African tribal ceremonies which often involved elaborate tattooing, with mud and coloring pounded into deep cuts.

"Deaden the skin? No, that's not possible. You're not a wimp, are you?"

MASCULINE STATUS

A tattoo allies its wearer—at least in his own mind—with the tough, the real, the macho. It represents the submerged desires of a large part of the male population. It leaves no doubt as to one's masculinity—according to the truckdriver with the bevy of girls decorating his pubic region.

The phenomenal success of the Marlboro cigarette campaigns in the 1950s and 1960s is something still remembered by the American male. Tough he-men and cowboys wore tattoos on the backs of hairy hands as they lighted a cigarette. Very probably there was much discussion in advertising offices before such a symbol was selected for a campaign, since tattoos were emblems of the outcast, the criminal—a dangerous association if you were addressing a non-criminal audience.

But the Marlboro campaign worked. Its unfortunate effects on tattoo artists and their customers did not matter: it sold cigarettes.

For a long time it made life difficult for us. Young men wanted a tattoo on the back of the hand. Ethical tattoo artists did not work on hands or faces, unless someone wanted a pachuco cross covered or had some other tattoo that had to be concealed. In vain did you tell stories about persons getting fired after they had their hands tattooed. Nor did anyone care that the Marlboro designs were simply inked on, and all of them upside-down so that they'd look right when the hand was held up to light the cigarette. I wouldn't tattoo the hand, but many unscrupulous jaggers up the street would. From the moment a person got a hand tattooed, his life was enormously complicated. Such tattoos could not be removed by ordinary surgical methods as others can, and skin grafts from the buttocks or thighs replaced the thin pliable covering of the back of the hand with a bulky hairless padding.

One particularly insistent person simply went to another tattooist and got an eagle on his hand. He came back about three months later and asked about the possibility of having it removed. He had been a waiter at the Ambassador East, one of Chicago's better hotels. But on the day he showed up with the eagle on his hand he had been fired, and had not been able to get a job since.

Andrew, an architectural draftsman from Indianapolis who never revealed his last name, got his torso covered down to the waist-line. He arrived every three weeks for work, having himself covered with a profusion of macaws, clipper-ships, swordfish, petals around the black center of his nipples, spiders with webs in his armpits, snakes wrapped around his arms, panthers, and a peacock—a very colorful guy when finished. He was cautious and polite and always had his wife with him. Whether this decoration of his body answered his deep desire to be the man his physical frame would never permit him to be, or whether afterwards he performed better in bed or let his wife lie unsatisfied while he masturbated, are — like the songs the mermaids sang or the name Achilles assumed when he hid himself among the women — puzzling matters but not beyond all conjecture.

AN EXISTENTIAL ACT

Eugene, one of my brighter former students at the university, once suggested that a tattoo constituted an existential act, one stemming from Sartre and Camus, and that perhaps the sailors and ex-cons anticipated the philosophy of Sartre. An existential act is one which is often completed in silence and alone, in anguish and despair, an act which once done is done forever. With some grim humor I always answered the question about how long a tattoo would last by saying: "They are guaranteed for life — and six months." I even pasted a sign to that effect on a small plastic skeleton that hung from the ceiling.

Though hardly any of my customers had ever heard the word existential, I had many times seen them tense at the end of a tattoo, flex the muscles, look at the completed design, and mutter something like: "By God, it's there for always." At such moments it was not wise to remind them that perhaps the tattoo *could* be removed. But even if it were, the memory of their forever act would always be with them in the form of a scar, or the tiny flecks of unremoved carbon under the skin. Such a thought — although unvoiced — could be seen or felt among hundreds of the young rebels without a cause . . . who got tattooed.

COMPENSATION

This is the great layman's psychiatric solution to all problems of emotional or physical insufficiency — everyman his own analyst, and his neighbor's as well. The tattoo seemed very popular as a device to relieve one's feelings of inferiority or one's loss of an arm or leg. Over eighteen years literally hundreds of maimed persons in wheelchairs or on crutches came for tattoos; and those who were mangled emotionally were even more numerous.

One of the first to appear was George — on crutches with both legs paralyzed, the result of a head-on collision of his motorcycle and a car. He had a fantastic hair-do, the middle front third of it hanging over his forehead and the sides brushed up and inwards, so that the forelock and sides looked somewhat like the Greek letter *omega*. He had an angular, chiseled face, and there was a deep scar on his left cheek. He reminded me of the anti-hero of Tennessee Williams' story "One Arm," and like that character George was also a hustler. He told many stories of his success in that line. Everyone wanted to give him money after one look at his crutches and that elegant suffering face of his. He carried around with him a little "advertising" booklet — polaroid shots of his genitals. "Saves time when you're hustlin' the queers," he said.

George's arms and chest were dense with small tattoos, for after every successful score he made, he came in to get another tattoo, usually a small bird or rose.

Deaf-mutes were also quite inclined towards tattoos, but never in large enough numbers for me to learn the sign language, so we communicated on notepaper. One day two came in: one of them had a crudely done name on his wrist and wanted it straightened. I did so, and when I had finished, he fainted without any preliminary warning signs. His friend was sitting across the room reading a comic book. I was caught — with one arm holding the guy to keep him off the floor and the other still holding the buzzing tattoo machine. I yelled at his buddy — to no avail. Finally I managed to put the needle down and pick up a pencil, which I threw. It hit him on the head; I signalled for some water — and at last we revived the unfortunate fellow, who had by then lost control of his bladder. It was not very funny to any of us.

One summer there appeared a sad little character with one leg. His name was Tony. He had difficulty working his crutches through the heavy door-check into the air-conditioned coolness of my shop. I went to help him, but he managed successfully. The empty trouser leg was neatly pinned high on his thigh.

"Damn, man," I said, "howja lose that?"

"Motorcycle accident," he said briefly.

Tony's story was that he hailed from Steubenville, Ohio, and wanted to become a tattoo artist. As a con-man he was enormously

Samuel M. Steward, PhD

talented. He fooled us all in the grand manner, and traded heavily on his infirmity. His leg had been gone about a year, he said, and he was saddled with a wife and two children. He looked so mournful and seemed so helpless that everyone took pity on him. Will you teach me how to become a tattoo artist? he wanted to know.

I was not about to teach anybody anything; I shuddered at the idea of even briefly returning to my former occupation. No, I said, but you can buy my correspondence course in tattooing for half price.

"Too much," he sighed. "I ain't got the dough. And you want too much for your professional lessons."

"Time's valuable," I said. "I can't tie myself up with teaching and miss customers when they come into the shop."

Then Tony said he was going to get a peddler's license and sell pencils in Chicago.

"Not allowed in the Loop," I said.

But Tony came back in three weeks with large stories of how he had been averaging $90 a day selling pencils in the Loop. One day he even made $400 dollars before the cops chased him away.

Or so he said. He was sending all the money home as fast as he could—and would I trust him for a tattoo? "I'll pay you as soon as I take in some more," he promised, and I agreed.

He finally disappeared, off on a wild wind to join a carnival in Wisconsin. I was out a considerable number of dollars and the price of four tattoos. In return I had a collection of several good stories about hobo life and con-men.

Whether the crippling was in the body or the mind, tattoos gave a good many unfortunates at least a temporary feeling of masculinity, and perhaps for a little while a feeling of being as good as any undamaged vessel.

IMITATION

This is such a large category that it might be considered a laundry bag for dumping everything—from the Marlboro advertisements to Robert Mitchum's mad preacher in *Night of the Hunter*. It might be made to include all the boys who would come in during the summer season—when the beaches were open and tattoos were visible—and say that they wanted a tattoo because they had seen one on somebody, usually a guy with a good "built." Such a category might be broken down into any number of other motivations—or perhaps it might be allowed to stand alone as a "pure" incentive: a guy wants a certain tattoo because he simply likes the appearance of it.

COMPULSION

Very early in my experience I began to notice a certain "addictiveness" to tattooing. If a guy got one tattoo, he very often wanted another. Once a city-boy asked me: "What do you put in those inks, Phil, that keeps us comin' back again and again?"

Without really thinking, I said, "Oh, a little dried dragon's blood and some mummy-dust. Those things are very habit-forming." The chance remark became a part of the standard patter in the shop. One gullible young man actually once returned especially to ask if I did put dragon's blood and mummy-dust into the colors.

"No," I said, with as straight a face as I could maintain, "not really, largely because it's very hard to find dragons nowadays."

He looked puzzled for a moment and then grinned widely. "Oh, I get it," he said, "there ain't no such thing as dragons."

"But there's lots of mummies," I said. "How's yours?"

We let it go at that.

The compulsion to get tattooed was in some people as strong an addiction as that to alcohol or perhaps a harder drug. Some are perfectly satisfied with one tattoo; others simply seem unable to stop. Often I came to consider a person who always returned to me for his tattoos as one of "my boys." Yet if he happened to be a compulsive—and my shop was closed—he would nonetheless go elsewhere and not wait for me.

Ken—who called himself a "big jackass mechanic"—was eager for me to get my new shop fixed up so that I could put a large rose on his chest. But I had to say not yet, because a carpenter had not finished making my slanted body bench. He stood the torment for two days, and then went elsewhere for an indifferent and poorly executed job. After that he was seized with a guilt reaction because of his "infidelity" to me, and stayed away for a long time. But he finally overcame his feelings and apologized profusely, after which

I put a large garland of flowers across his massive back, and for-
gave him — especially after he insisted on paying me double.

Paul, an executive from New York, often visited me when he
passed through Chicago. He was one of the most compulsive cases I
had ever seen. He was big-boned and almost completely covered
with tattoos. It grew so strong in him that he even got a set of
needles and colors and had cards printed — all this after tattooing
had been made illegal in New York City. He really lost his mind
when he saw a tattoo shop or saw anyone getting tattooed. For a
long time he kept his parents from knowing about his obsession; his
shirt cuffs were always buttoned tightly about his wrists.

Paul was about forty, and the tattoo had for him become so inti-
mately associated with sex that the mere sight of a design on a sailor
would set him trembling. After a few drinks all self-control vanished. I had often cautioned him against a tattoo on his hand —
which he wanted desperately. But one night in San Francisco he
saw a sailor getting such a tattoo from an unscrupulous artist, and
he succumbed, getting a bird on each palm. His remorse the next
day was almost suicidal.

But some small bit of control was forced on Paul. The New York
police got hold of one of his cards and wanted to search his apartment. In great fright he stashed all his equipment with friends in
Chicago, refused to answer his phone or doorbell, and was in general traumatized sufficiently to teach him a lesson. But the compulsion was merely suppressed for a while, not removed.

Another New Yorker, "Harry Smith" — quite wealthy — decided
that instead of another Cadillac he would get his whole body tattooed. He owned his own firm, the only one in the world manufacturing one special kind of earth-moving equipment. Harry was an
exhibitionist and also involved in the early "leather movement."
He got himself totally covered by certain tattoo artists operating
outside the city limits. And then it was all over, finished, done. He
had no more skin to cover. Undaunted, he decided that he would
have everything blacked out except certain favorite gaudy designs
on torso and legs. The tattoos, however, began to slip down on his
hands — small stars and flowers between the fingers and on the
palms.

I remonstrated with him. "Harry," I said, "in your position this is something which you ought not to let happen. What will your clients say?"

Twinkling, Harry replied, "Well, if they don't want to do business with me they'll just have to buy from another firm"—a wry statement, since his was the only firm manufacturing that particular equipment.

Once, in a mimeographed Navy publication, a Catholic Navy chaplain said that one tattoo was "all right" for a sailor but more than one made him "emotionally suspect." Just what the asshole meant by this would be very difficult to define.

There was compulsion enough in myself in the early days of tattooing. I designed a garland of flowers reaching from one shoulder-peak to the other, with a large rose in the center, feeling that a tattoo artist should be tattooed. Dietzel in Milwaukee put it on, in three sessions—with a year between each. A whimsy on my part made me get the three parts of it on three successive Good Fridays.

But suddenly and actively thrusting myself into the game as a businessman very quickly killed the urge to decorate myself. The death of my "romance" with tattooing was brought about simply by overwork. The flood of sailors and civilians quickly ended the glamour and mystique of tattooing. It could not survive the fatigue of long hours seven days a week, nor the endless answering of stupid questions about it—the same ones over and over.

CELEBRATION

A small but amusing grouping, noticed on very few occasions and made up only of those who had already been tattooed. Some young man might burst into the shop, lark-happy. Usually it was someone I had seen before.

"Phil, I just dis minnit got outa th' pokey!" he might say. "Been in a year for—" well, take your pick: anything from rape to grand theft . . . "an' I gotta have sumpin to celebrate! How's about a comin'-out tattoodle?"

I could never see much difference between such euphoric statements and a woman's desire to buy a new hat.

"ALIVENESS"

Aside from the masochist's enjoyment of the needle, there was another aspect to the *feel* of getting a tattoo. A handsome little blond heterosexual named "Bimbo" once gave me the clue. He had a great many tattoos, most of which he had got from me. But on this one occasion—while I was working on a dragon on his forearm, he suddenly looked up at me with eyes shining and said, "Gee, Phil! I like that needle! It makes me feel so alive!"

This sense of existing, of feeling, of enjoying life, came to many with the touch of the needle, and not merely the compulsives. It was simply a generalized euphoria which increased with the progress of the tattoo. Perhaps some of the feeling of "aliveness" came from a masochistic pleasure, but not all. Had Bimbo and his kind been gifted with the talent of a Walt Whitman, they would have been writing down their impressions about the general joy of living, of feeling, of existing. This is not an observation born of romanticism. It was noticed often and emphatically enough to merit its mention as a very genuine motivation.

NON-CONFORMITY AND REBELLION

A typical juvenile delinquent, a native Chicagoan gang-member, once asked me to design for him a tattoo of a motorcycle boot crushing a policeman's cap. It turned out to be quite attractive. I put it on the kid before I began to think much about it. When the cops eventually picked him up—and they were sure to do so one day— they would no doubt whale the daylights out of him (this was in the 1950s, remember) when they saw such an anti-police tattoo. It was a true symbol of the rebellion of the young against authority. Then it would occur to some wise fuzz to ask where the guy had got it, and the kid would surely tell, for despite all the big talk, there was not one of the young men who could stand up against the police methods when he faced them alone. And if he talked, then I would be in trouble. I removed the design from my flash, and put it on only once thereafter in Chicago, on a masochist from New York who was too old and timid to get into police difficulties. But later in

California, it turned out to be one of the most popular ones put on the Hells (no apostrophe) Angels.

The terms "conformity" and "non-conformity" are only relative. In any segment of society such as the Navy where most of the members have a tattoo, the thing itself becomes a symbol of conformity, of following the crowd, of the herd-instinct. In another segment, however, where all skin is unmarked, the tattoo becomes a symbol of non-conformity. When hippies first appeared, beards and longhair and sandals were non-conformity symbols, but soon these marks of defiance became the commonplace signs of group-membership.

For many of the customers the tattoo was definitely a sign of the anti-social "rebels without a cause." Some of them dimly blamed their elders or parents or the police, whereas many were simply rebelling vaguely against the world. They felt everyone was against them, although why they did not know, or how. In the 1960s I did not tattoo many love-children; some got small flowers here and there. I remained rather aloof from the hippie philosophy, largely because I had lived all my life in rebellion against authority of several kinds. Listening to their shallow spoutings gave me the feeling of having to sit through the same movie twice. Perhaps this was due to my having been nearly expelled from a state university for starting a "movement" to integrate sororities and fraternities long before the civil rights struggles began. My own white horse was early stabled and the banners furled, and the "philosophies" of the 1960s seemed more repetitive than illuminating.

Part of this feeling of rebellion is anti-intellectual. Since a tattoo to certain levels of society is the mark of a thug, it becomes also the sign of inarticulate revolt, often producing its only possible result — violence. And many upper-class masochists found that a tattoo brought them the continuing psychic humiliation they desired.

Some of this anti-intellectual feeling appeared in myself. As I sank deeper and deeper into the cut-throat world, odd changes began to take place. The "street" suddenly seemed to be more like home. When I passed under the elevated tracks and entered the honky-tonk world, I felt more at ease — a strange psychic change. I breathed more freely and felt better. And of course my language changed. I floored many customers with big words occasionally, but I began to talk more like the delinquents, using their own language to them, plentifully garnished with four-letter words and obscenities. That was what they liked. They felt right at home.

GANG MEMBERSHIP

During the 1950s literally thousands of young men who had never been near a real "pachuco" inscribed the webs of their left hands with the pachuco mark, a simple cross with three rays. This movement, originating among the Mexican gangs of southern California, spread like wildfire across the country, antedating the hippies and the Hells Angels. It caused a scandal in the Air Force in the mid-1950s, with many airmen dismissed because of it; and was for many years a cause for police questioning when it was seen on the hand or elsewhere. It was my strict policy never to tattoo the hands unless cover-work were demanded, but I did disguise thousands of pachuco marks, changing them into small flowers or anchors with three stars.

Several of the Chicago gangs developed their own designs and made half-hearted attempts to have each member wear the symbol on their arms. These designs were usually crude, primitive, and unattractive; and after putting on a dozen or more of them, I was usually faced with the problem of later covering them with another design. I made a small black bear for the "Bearcats," a cocktail glass with a tiny red cherry for the "Manhattans," a stylized wildcat for the "Valiants"—one of the most troublesome of the local gangs. The "Road-Wolves" who had early descended on me never had the intelligence nor the inclination to design their own symbol.

When I opened my shop in California, after the Illinois legislature prevented the tattooing of persons under twenty-one, I soon discovered that I was in the heartland of the outlaw motorcycle club, the Hells Angels. But in one way I was lucky, One of the group found me early, a fellow who because of his past ministerial experience, was called "Saint Luke." He was an intelligent guy with a large frame and he wore many tattoos, including all the favored designs of the club. He looked at my clean new shop and shook his head sadly.

"I think I'd better keep the rest of the guys out of here," he said in his slow way.

"Why for?" I asked, always a man with a nose for a buck.

"They're too loud and noisy," he said. "They'd drink in here — "

" — not in this shop," I said.

"Too cruel anywhere," he replied with a line from *Macbeth*. "Well, then, they'd come in already drunk and stomp around and raise hell generally. And where and when they come, the cops are right behind."

"I guess you're right," I said. "I reckon I can do without them."

They found me later, however, in large numbers, and until I closed my shop in 1970 I was in a sense the "official" tattoo artist for them, some of whom came to Oakland from as far away as San Bernardino and elsewhere. By the time they found me Saint Luke had already told me the meanings of their various patches and designs: DFFL, which meant "Dope Forever, Forever Loaded"; and AFFA, Angels Forever, Forever Angels." The famous "1%" marking enclosed in a black-outlined red-shaded diamond lozenge referred to the statement of the American Motorcycle Association that "only 1% of motorcycle riders in the States are outlaws." I put on Saint Luke the Chinese lettering for "Angels [belonging to] Hell," as well as a large black swastika and the figure "13" enclosed in a lozenge; the "13" referred to the thirteenth letter of the alphabet, but there was some dispute whether the "M" stood for marijuana or masochist.

Other symbols which the Saint explained were an Air Force patch with the wings reddened and a red circle at their juncture, meaning that an Angel had performed cunnilingus on a menstruating woman; the same design with a black circle meant the Angel preferred boys or had jackrolled homosexuals, or been a hustler. Multiple meanings allowed several possible exits from accusations.

One of the latest marks was "666," the number of the Beast in the Apocalypse. Saint Luke said that a southern Baptist minister in a sermon denouncing the gang had told his congregation in horrified tones: "They are tattooed with the number of the Beast — 666!" Luke saw this in the newspaper and told Sonny Barger, president of the mother-club; the two decided that if the minister said so, it must be true—and from that moment 666 became a favored mark of the gang.

Gang-marks never became as popular in the United States as they were in France and England, or in Singapore's secret society. Interpol in August, 1965, had a definitive article in its monthly publication on gang tattoos, but with the exception of the Hells Angels American gangs seemed more short-lived than other gangs of the world-scene.

FETISHISM

It would perhaps take many hours on a psychiatrist's couch to find the subconscious roots of this reaction, and the difficulty of making any analysis is great. But there seemed to be many examples of it among my customers.

Early evidence of it came with John, who had been an official of a major oil company. Most of the persons who might be termed fetishists in tattooing were extremely intelligent, and were either towards the top in a social hierarchy or well-placed in the business world.

John was a tattoo buff, but had only one or two on himself. He was fascinated with the idea of tattooed women. Every time he came into the Chicago shop he wanted to know what women had been tattooed recently. His questioning at last became tiresome, and I began to make up stories to satisfy him. His reactions were possibly like those of a person making an obscene phone call. The more I talked, the more his eyes would glitter and he would become sexually aroused—or mentally excited. He finally married a French girl and compelled her to get many floral tattoos around her celestial gate.

Bob was a district sales manager for a major appliance company, hard of hearing and rather dull mentally, but in his late thirties he still had the ashes of a good body and handsome face. Like John, he was continually pestering me for details about the women I had tattooed; the glitter of arousal was as evident in him as it was in John. His particular interest lay in tattoos on women's feet—and there were not many tales to tell him about that.

Finally—Mr. Karl. An odd character walked into the shop one

busy Saturday when the place was full of sailors. He was about sixty and had a decided limp. He talked rather drunkenly about getting a tattoo, but since I was working at full speed on sailors who had waited a long time, I paid little attention. At last when the shop was empty I could listen. He had a fetish for women's shoes and he wanted a couple of full girl-figures on him—not nudes—but the high heels had to be just so. He ended by getting three.

A few nights later a woman called and asked if Karl were there. She described him and said that she was his daughter, and told me that he was a surgeon who had had a breakdown and was under psychiatric care and would I please not tattoo him again. She added that after the session with me he had come home, weeping copiously with remorse over his "forever" act.

I can understand why parents give in to begging children. Mr. Karl came back again and again, always asking for girls in high-heeled shoes. I told him of the conversation with his daughter, but in his gentle way he persuaded me that he was cured, and that she complained simply because she was prejudiced against tattoos.

At last I succumbed. This time he wanted his penis scaled in green, like a snake or a fish. This I undertook. Never again. The topskin moves this way and that; many times when I thought I had finished, the skin scooted around once more and revealed yet another uncompleted square inch. Finally I said: "Your women will scream and leap from bed when they see this thing."

"Aw Phil," he said, "don't say that or you'll make me sorry I had it done."

"I think you were foolish to ask for it at all," I said, overstepping my early resolve never to be surprised or critical of anyone's fantasies or whimsies in a tattoo shop.

When I moved from Chicago to California, word reached me that Cliff Raven—one of the guys I started on the tattooed path—inherited Mr. Karl, whose high-heeled girls had been mostly blacked out in great blotches by then. At a loss about what to do with him, Cliff finally turned him into an abstract piece of cubist art which—although interesting—was not purchased by any museum.

There were about twelve of these puzzle-people paying regular visits, always with tongue hanging out for any information they could get about women and tattoos. I never could get any real answers from them about their fetishes. The shade was obviously pulled down. At one point John said rather hesitantly, "Well, I suppose it's a form of fetishism."

"Oh, thanks for the illumination," I said, sardonically. "But it must certainly be more than that. How could a mere fetish be so powerful? Does it make you feel more manly? Can you trace it back to its origin? In what area does it really operate best?"

"It would take quite a while to find out," said John, grinning. "And why bother? Why not just say that I enjoy seeing them on women and hearing about them?"

The sources of the appeal that tattooed women had for men probably went far beyond fetishism. Thousands of times there were questions from sailors and city-boys, always the same: "Do women come in here to get tattooed?"

"Yes," I would say. "Tramps and dykes. Nice girls don't get tattooed."

"Where do they get it?"

My answer was always the same: "Right where you're thinking. Tits also? Yes. But that's like tattooing a bowlful of Jello. Or mush." And then if it happened to be a friendly group I would tell the story of the woman who wanted a swallow-tail butterfly tattooed down alongside her port of entry.

"You see," I'd say. "She wanted that swallow-tailed butterfly right down there, with one tail going down each side of it. Well, you know you have to stretch the skin tight to get the needle in," and here I would demonstrate on the arm of the boy who was getting tattooed. "But I couldn't get hold of her, nothing to grab onto. I pulled and struggled for a while and then I looked at her and said: 'You'll really have to excuse me—this is the only way I can get it done.' And with that I put two fingers in and pushed out, and that way I got it finished."

General laughter. Pandemonium. Whacking of thighs. Ah, the stories that are told in the friendly old tattoo shop!

PASTIMES

Tattooing is often merely a pastime, either in prison or at home. Boys too young to visit a professional shop will tattoo themselves, wrapping three needles with thread and buying a bottle of "Indian" ink. They put the crudest sorts of designs on their arms, only to have to come in when they are older to have the lettering or tattooing "straightened." It is usually an impossibility to improve their lopsided writing; sometimes the only solution is a cover-up. Since they do not know the skin has to be taut, each pin-prick is widely spaced — a collection of black dots. Temporary tattoos were not to be invented until the 1970s — decals which stayed a few days and which could be easily removed.

In the pokey, however, the case is different. Time hangs heavy. Nothing to do. The prisoners steal some needles and thread from the tailor shop. For ink they burn a candle against the cement ceiling and scrape off the soot, or they burn toilet paper and crumble the ashes in water. Either way they get pure carbon, which is after all the basis for the professional tattooist's black ink. Neither this pure carbon, however, or ordinary "India" ink is stabilized with the addition of iron oxide, and consequently turns blue after a little while.

Then after lights are out — because tattooing is generally forbidden in prisons — the two cell-mates will crawl under the blankets, and one will painfully and sometimes elaborately tattoo his buddy. I saw thousands of "pokey" tattoos and began to ask what happened after the tattoo was finished. About eight out of ten would answer "Nuthin'" until I bluntly asked: "And then did you jack each other off?"

Affirmative response: very large number of instances. They would either admit it somewhat shamefacedly, or else say: "Gah-damn, how did you know?"

The blanket, the darkness, the needles and the pain, the secrecy and rule-breaking, the sense of danger, the heat from their bodies, and — perhaps — the very idea of tattooing all contributed to a sexual arousal, and masturbation proved the easiest way out. The continuing investigations of sex in prison establish the fact that activities other than masturbation probably took place as well.

UTILITARIAN

A rather small category, whose members wanted some kind of identification on their bodies in case of accident; or to enable them, as one drunk once said to me, getting his Social Security number tattooed on his arm to "cash my welfare checks without any trouble."

A Chicago doctor, Andrew Ivy, was once seized with a brilliant idea, advocated in the media, "have everyone tattooed with his blood type, name, and Social Security number so that if there's an atom bomb explosion it will be much easier to identify the bodies."

After much thought, the doctor decided that somewhere inconspicuously on the trunk of the body would be the optimal place, since arms and legs might be blown off. Ah—the ribs! preferably on the left side! would be the least visibly annoying.

He launched his campaign. It fell flat. One or two customers asked for it, but no more. The reason? Any tattoo artist could have told him. He had unwittingly picked the second most painful part of the body for his inscription. The first customer who got it on the ribs fainted dead away before I even got the blood type on him. Then word must have got around because there very were few after that.

Only a few hundred persons had their numbers or full names tattooed on themselves. The purely utilitarian motive was very slight indeed. One said he feared amnesia. Another was sensitive to penicillin, and such information was duly recorded on the upper quadrant of his buttocks, right where the needle goes in.

The physician's wife, she of whom her husband had said that her tattoos were more beautiful to him than diamonds, also claimed they made identification easier. When she would order airline tickets by phone in her home town in Washington State, her name would mean nothing until she added—"You know, the tattooed lady." Then there was an immediate response from the clerk. This, she said, she found very helpful. Perhaps so, but I thought the motive spurious and was sure that the basic reasons lay deeper, and were undoubtedly in the category of "none of your business."

Dr. Robert L. Dickinson, one of the real sexual pioneers preceding Kinsey, once made interesting use of the utilitarian motive. He had his index finger tattooed with inch-marks so that he could easily measure the depth of female entry canals.

In a related vein, I once tattooed inch-marks on a gay male. He wanted them put on the inner side of his left forearm, with his hand held out in a straight extension of the arm, palm upwards. The first mark, at five inches, was a short red line at the base of the palm on the little finger side, the second at six inches, and three, four, and five -- down to ten inches -- running up the side of the forearm. Thus he always had at hand a convenient ruler to measure objects in which he was interested. Only rarely did he find anything that exceeded his built-in measuring-stick. Although these marks were applied in the mid 1950s, they were still visible in the 1990s on the side of my arm.

GUILT AND PUNISHMENT

People in our modern society seem to be harassed and guilt-ridden to an amazing degree; it would be unusual if there were not some reflection of these feelings in tattooing, since -- like a looking-glass -- it reflects so many other facets of the personality.

There is -- an abundance. One Mexican boy came in and wanted a head of Christ on his arm. I was considerably shocked [but not visibly moved] to see that from shoulder to wrist his arm was heavily striated with deep knife scars.

"I'm bad," he murmured. "I punish myself."

Why conceal your inner burden of guilt when you can display it disguised on your arm? The old French criminal motto, *La Mort Avant le Déshonneur*, transferred to the American Navy and thence sinking down to the hoodlum element, often reappeared in the many "Death Before Dishonor" tattoos that were applied. It was to be found usually on ex-cons, or on sailors or soldiers who had received bad conduct discharges. One sailor had me reverse the words and put "Dishonor before Death" on his arm. It got him discharged from the Navy; the brass decided they didn't like his attitude. Pangs of conscience wormed inside me until I learned that he really had wanted to be out of the service. I sometimes asked a civilian smartass who had got the Death Before Dishonor skull and dagger: "What does that really mean to you? Does it mean that you'd rather be killed than fucked in the ass?" Nearly all of them were shocked to realize what might be the actual meaning of the words. One person did, however, and had me immediately conceal the lettering with small flowers.

A favorite pastime of the guilt-ridden is self-mutilation -- witness

Oedipus blinding himself, or the Hemingway character who emasculated himself [ah there, Ernest!] to remove the agency of his sin. But when you can absolve yourself by getting the right tattoo, or do penance in a way which does not loudly declare your guilt, why carry your bed of nails around with you? A tattoo answers the purpose effectively for the guilt-ridden masochist. The adulterer gets his wife's name under a rose on his arm; it hurts; he is punished by a small pain for his infidelity to her.

The motto "Born To Lose," inscribed under a little red "Hot Stuff" devil with a pitchfork, or a small Disney skunk, was very popular with ex-convicts and those who in self-pity felt that life had given them a dirty deal.

One customer was a notorious Don Juan. Every time he bedded a woman other than his wife, he came in for a tattoo; he was literally covered with small inconsequential designs, and had his wife's name on him in at least twenty places. I asked if he did not feel the repetition somewhat overdid it for him. He shrugged.

"It's easier to give you a coupla bucks," he said, "than to go to confession."

That reminded me that in some Arab countries you can earn forgiveness for a night of sin by dropping a few coins into the cup of the first beggar you see the next morning. It's the easiest way, and it doesn't hurt the conscience at all.

ADVERTISEMENT

Most of the tattoos in this grouping were in some way sexual — either advertising what the person wanted, or what he was. On one man — evidently a cut above the average — I wrote "Don Juan." On another: "Noli me tangere" [Do not touch me]; it turned out that he was such a Protestant fundamentalist that he had never had a sexual experience of any kind. On another person's ankle I put a rose, around which were four Chinese characters: "Man," "wants" [desires], "penis," "to suck" [to be sucked], a formula which took in a good deal of territory. He later returned to tell me of some wild adventures he had in the Alexian Brothers hospital with a Chinese intern.

It was a fad in the 1940s and 1950s to have tattooed on the base joints of the fingers of one hand the letters: L T F C, and on the other hand to have: E S U K. Then the person with such lettering could hold his hands, palms downward with fingers interleaved, to convey his message. I saw several examples of this in the shop and even had requests for it, which I refused because of my policy never to tattoo anything on the hands unless it were cover-work.

On one masochist's shoulder I put a whip, with the initials "S" and "M" worked into the coils of the braiding. Within the pubic hair of a male hooker I put the figure of "$10"; what he did about that after inflation eroded the dollar's value I never learned. Above the mons veneris of a whore I wrote "Pay as You Enter."

In a large sense, it may be presumed that any tattoo is an advertisement of some kind: symbols of death and violence such as skulls or daggers were popular with misfits and rebels. Comic tattoos may have been intended to proclaim a certain insincerity about the tattoo—an attempt to ridicule the act itself, to make the tattoo less conspicuously important to others while it remained *very* important to the wearer; to treat the whole thing as an ironic joke, a matter of no consequence at all.

SENTIMENTALITY

Thousands of young men got hearts or roses with "Mom" inscribed in the accompanying banner. Three elements seemed to be involved in this: the growth of "Momism"—possibly the least potent; actual sentimental love for their mothers—which may have been the majority reason; or finally—to "soften up" the "old lady," to alter her reaction at seeing a new tattoo from fury to a "Oh-now-isn't-that-sweet-and-thoughtful." Those who got the current girl-friend's name in it made a mistake, but there's hardly any way to talk a person out of puppy love.

Another kind of sentimentality involved the name of one's home state, or the outline of it. It became a kind of link with home, a moral support in soldiers and sailors on their way to foreign wars.

Other memorialists wanted to have a tattoo from every place in the world where they had visited. Such persons were usually sailors, but now and then you found a tattoo buff who made quite a point of it—a small crown from London, a wooden shoe from Holland, a harp or a shamrock from Ireland, the Eiffel Tower from Paris. Sometimes it was merely the name of the country. Larry, the early acquaintance who led me into tattooing, once took a round-the-world trip and returned with the names of some twenty countries inscribed in their national alphabets on the inside of his left biceps.

Veterans of wars would sometimes come in — long afterwards, to be sure — to have the initials of the Army or Navy put on them somewhere, together with their long-unused serial numbers or ship or battalion names.

On the other hand, I was certain that many persons faked their travels or past military connections merely to impress their friends, or to create for themselves in their own minds the same kind of darkly romantic past that made Othello attractive to sheltered Desdemona.

BRAVADO, BRAGGADOCCIO, AND "WICKEDNESS"

It was not unusual for one boy to dare another to get a tattoo. Many young men would never have got one, but were unable to withstand the peer pressure when within the group. "You're chicken-shit if you don't" was heard very often, and few were able to withstand the challenge. "I'm braver than you are," was the unspoken taunt.

Others brought their girl-friends with them. As much as possible I discouraged this, for it often resulted in the boy getting a tattoo he didn't really want, just to impress the girl, like Tom Sawyer showing off in front of Becky Thatcher. Such braggadoccio sometimes misfired, however, when the boy got woozy or came near fainting in front of his lady-fair. At such times, much against his protests that he was all right — and he sitting there as pale as grandmother's old bedsheet, with sweat pouring off his forehead — I would have to hold his head down between his legs with pressure, a position from which he arose silent and furious, with me and with himself. But his anger was a small price to pay to avoid going for mop and bucket to clean up the mess.

There were some who came into the shop just to look around,

and then decided to get one "just for the hell of it" and to be "wicked." Mixed with such a motivation might be any one or several of those already considered. Some might be merely impulse-motivated or moved merely by boredom. Sometimes I heard such expressions of motive as: "Cheez, we was sittin' around wit' nuthin' to do and somebody says 'Let's go down to Phil's and get us a tatt or two, so here we are.'"

MAGIC AND TOTEMISM

In the old days of sailing vessels, sailors used to have "H-O-L-D F-A-S-T" tattooed on their hands, one letter to each finger, as a kind of magic protection against falling into the sea when they had to climb the rigging. Modern sailors sometimes want a pig tattooed on the dorsal arch of one foot, and a rooster on the other. The theory is that since these two animals are notable for their inability to swim, they would make for land as hard and fast as they could if they went overboard. These are primitive magics like the tattoo of the winged phallus, originating in Italy, which is supposed to enable a man to have an erection when it is most needed. A few Americans wear this design today.

On one Scandinavian I once placed a set of Druidic runes which signified (so he said): "Victory over my enemies." Another, a light-skinned black, got what he said was a mystic voodoo design guaranteed to protect him from evil and bring success in love.

There seem not to be many persons left in the world of tattoo who believe in the "mystic" powers of their designs, but even so, there is one curious kind of extension of this category of "magic," long before the advent of the self-healing "arts" of the 1960s: transactional meditation, biofeedback, or other mind-over-matter fads and fancies.

Occasionally some weak-minded soul would come into the shop and complain of being troubled by something—in one case, a fear of cancer returning after an operation. He believed that if I tattooed an open wound on his belly, an open gash out of which came tumbling various nuts and bolts, he would be relieved of his fears every time he looked at it. Another one, threatened by his father with a blow-torch aimed at his genitals [to stop his habit of masturbating], "cured" himself by having a blow-torch tattooed on his lower groin, similarly pointed at the father of all evil.

While teasing a friend of mine who believed implicitly in such mental mechanisms, I commented that he had hardly enough skin area to hold all the totems which would relieve every one of his difficulties; he responded with: "Oh, I think I'd need only one design — a tombstone with your name on it."

Another score for the common man.

RELIGION, CONSECRATION, STIGMATA, AND THE MESSIAH COMPLEX

Sometimes overly religious persons asked for designs of Christ on the cross, heads of Christ, crowns of thorns, or bleeding hearts. A priest in Milwaukee was almost covered with religious designs; on him I placed several. He had written a piece of quasi-mystic prose about the religious significance of his designs, one of the silliest things ever put in print.

Other than devout persons and those who asked for Biblical quotations, there was a mysterious group of religiously inclined persons who did not understand their motives for wanting tattoos. Perhaps if they secretly yearned for martyrdom, or bleeding palms with the stigmata, or nocturnal visions or the ability to teleport themselves to Rome in an eye-twinkle, might they not have thought they could make these things happen — or something close to the magical-mystical — by getting a tattoo?

A very odd cross-eyed boy came in once and asked for a head of Christ on his biceps. He picked out one I had never liked; it always rather irreverently reminded me of a 16th century Italian nobleman straining at stool. But he got it — crown of thorns, blood drops, red-robed collar and all. He seemed very pleased with it and said as he looked at it: "Do you think I could get a priest to bless it?"

"Why not?" I said. "After all, they bless motorcycles."

But I never learned whether he succeeded in finding someone to do it.

NATIONAL AND/OR ETHNIC ORIGINS

Closely allied with the motivation of sentimentality but slightly different was the small class of patriots who wanted a symbol of their country of origin. The harp and shamrock with "Erin Go Bragh" (often misspelled by illiterate jaggers) was used for the professional Irishman, and some of the genuine ones. The maple-leaf was put on Canadians, the fleur-de-lys on Frenchmen, and the distinctive boot-outline of Italy on Italians. Quite a few Mexicans wanted the eagle-serpent-and-cactus of their national flag.

There were not many symbols available to patriotic citizens of the United States. Only once did I have a request for the hammer and sickle of Russia, and only three times (before the Hells Angels) for the swastika. Two of the three Nazi symbols were later covered up, one in great haste by an empty-headed redneck who belatedly discovered that his employer was Jewish.

Young sailors often asked for the Confederate flag — as a bulwark against the tauntings of their damn-yankee buddies. One ignorant young swabbie from Georgia asked insistently for a Navy design which in its usual form carried the U.S. flag above an eagle perched on an anchor, and a banner which was supposed to carry the initials U.S.N. He wanted the U.S. flag changed to the Confederate one, but I refused, pointing out the illogic of "USN" under a Confederate flag.

"Make it CSAN," I said, "for the Confederated States of America, and I'll do it." His buddies laughed at him a good deal, and he finally settled for the American flag with USN.

And then of course there were the Texans, wanting — needless to say — the Lone Star flag or the yellow rose.

PART V

The Folklore of Tattooing

There has perhaps been more misinformation about tattooing and tattoos than about any other single game, occupation, or pastime on the American scene.

The rumors, half-facts, and downright untruths arise from two sources: the clientele and the tattoodlers themselves. The world of tattoo is dim and mysterious to most persons. There is a human tendency to create misinformation about something not understood; all kinds of "logical" stories are made up about tattooing, and then given support by use of the familiar phrase: "I knew a guy who . . ."

But the main source of the malarkey about tattooing is the tattoo artists' themselves. They are not on the whole extremely intelligent; most of them do not know *why* the pigments remain permanently in the skin, nor do they understand the diffusion of the pigments into the neighbor cells—which causes not only blurring after a few years but makes the tattoo extremely difficult to remove (except by skin graft or laser) after a period of three years. Nor do most tattoo artists know to what depth they place the pigment, nor where it rests— whether in corium, melanin layer, bottom of the dermis, the producing cells or the papillae.

Neither do most know exactly why the pigment itself is not absorbed or digested by the skin. The answer to that is simple: the pigments are inert metallic chemicals; the skin tries to eject them as a foreign substance during the healing process. That failing, it grows a thin cyst layer beneath the pigments, and then gives up and leaves them alone. The permanence of a tattoo is one good way of scotching another ancient bit of folklore: that the body cells are changed completely or replaced every seven years. If they were the

81

tattoo would disappear completely. Old Randy in the arcade shop insisted that a tattoo cured syphilis. Possibly in his dim way he had heard of an article in the *Journal of the American Medical Association* stating that a syphilitic ulcer on a man's arm, originating on his wrist and traveling upwards, was stopped dead when it reached the red pigment of a tattoo. No wonder: the red pigment was a spirocheticide — mercuric sulfide, one of the old specifics against syphilis before the days of penicillin. The presence of mercury in the skin was enough to arrest the progress of a shallow skin ulcer; after that, the bugs went undercover.

Not understanding the *why* of many things, then, the tattoo artists — gifted with the wondrous imaginations of con-men — are very quick to create logical-sounding stories about the art itself.

Some of the magic values of tattoos have already been mentioned — that the winged phallus tattoo will assure the wearer great sexual powers, that a pig or rooster on the foot will keep the wearer from drowning. A circled "x" will protect the bearer from accidents in moving vehicles. Such examples are set forth in perfect seriousness, even though they are the purest examples of primitive magics. Old Randy had a voodoo symbol which he assured me guaranteed success in love to the one who wore it. Years of listening to such hogwash makes it difficult to believe that one lives in a scientifically-oriented society in the twentieth century. What you hear in a tattoo shop reminds you of the arcane information you might get from a medieval alchemist.

The misinformation largely concerns three categories: removing tattoos, legendary tattoos, and how to care for a new tattoo. The truth for the last: leave it alone and keep it as dry as possible.

The removal category of fables is the most hilarious and outrageous. During my tattoo years perhaps two hundred substances were trumpeted as sure-fire means of removing tattoos. It was always a friend who had it done, although several brazen ones showed me an unmarked arm and swore that a tattoo had been removed from that particular spot. Obviously not — because even with surgical removal some faint trace remains, or hair does not grow, or the melanin color-layer is disturbed and the skin won't tan.

The favorite removal substances were almost always obnoxious. You were supposed to tattoo them into the design. Some were traditional: "My buddy took off his tattoo with a needle and lemon juice." Lemon juice would have no effect on metallic tattoo pigments. Nor would chlorine. Put some color into a commercial chlorine—much stronger than the household kind—and leave for two weeks. At the end of that time the color is as bright and unbleached as the day it was put in.

Another substance that had a popular and sterling reputation for removal was mother's milk, with goat's milk a close second. From here the list goes down the path, to pregnant mare's urine and others, each more exotic than the last.

A sailor came into the Chicago shop once and started talking about removals. Before long he said, "I had a buddy once who took a tattoo off with shark gyzym."

I laughed and choked. He was nonplused.

"How in the world did he get hold of some of that?" I finally managed to say. "Did he swim out into shark-infested waters and capture one? Very dangerous."

The gullible kid looked a little startled. "Chee," he said, "I never thought of that."

"And how," I asked, boring in, "did he get the shark to hold still long enough to get it? Did he bring a female shark along to get him all excited? And do sharks have a penis so that he could jack it off? And how could he get the real stuff without having it mixed with sea water'

The poor boy started to turn red, one of the most magnificent blushes ever. "Jus' wait until I get hold of that sonofabitch," he muttered, looking ferocious.

"Don't believe everything you hear," I told him.

But people do. No one knows where the old stories started— likely with some bored or annoyed tattoo artist, for we all get tired of answering the endless questions. And then the disinformation is spread through the pages of the popular men's magazines which clutter the news stands.

As soon as you told anyone that tattoos had to be removed surgically, the kids knew all about it. "Yeah," they would say, "an' it costs _____ a square inch," filling in the blank with anything from $11.00 to $300.00.

My reply to such statements was usually the same: "What would you do if a doctor took out a ruler and measured it while you were there and said 'Yes, it's fourteen dollars a square inch'? I tell you what I'd do—I'd get the hell out of that office because I'd know he was a quack.''

''Well, then—'' somewhat belligerently. ''How much do they cost?''

''Depends on the doctor,'' I said, ''and whether he has to take it off by skin graft or dermabrasion.''

''Wot's that?''

''The same way they smooth down acne scars,'' I said. ''They use a rapidly revolving brush with plastic bristles on a drill like a dentist's. The doctor deadens the arm [I had long since stopped saying ''anesthetize''], hangs up a plastic sheet and lets fly. You have a bad scar for a while, but if it's done properly the hair grows back and it still tans. Sometimes the doc uses a long-bladed vibrating knife. But it has to be done by an expert.''

''A skin graft is better though, ain't it?''

''Not necessarily,'' I said. ''If it's been put in deep or is older than three years, you'll have to have a skin graft made. But then you'll have a scar on your butt where the skin came from, as well as one on your arm. And it always looks different. The hair pattern ain't the same.''

''A cover-up job is better and cheaper then, ain't it?''

''Yeah. But sometimes you can't do that. You couldn't cover a black panther, for instance, because only black covers black. You'd have to have a covering design where you can shade the new black over the old black and still have it look right.''

Old Shaky Jake's method of removal, mentioned before, was dangerous and expensive. The keratolytic agents he used—salicylic or tannic acid or both—never worked the first time; you had to go back, and at $25 to $50 a crack it got expensive. If the removal did succeed without infection, it left a dead-white puffy scar that resembled a bas-relief vaccination mark.

A fat youngster who wanted an athletic scholarship at a small religious school in Wisconsin found that he could not get it because of his tattoos. He decided to have them removed and found a Wisconsin doctor to do the work, a man who quite evidently knew nothing about such things. He made deep incisions to the bottom of the dermis, about a quarter of an inch, cut off the whole tattoo and then pulled the skin tightly together and sewed it. The resulting scars were abominable, looking much worse than the tattoos.

The young man returned several years later with hideously scarred arms, and I asked him how he made out with his athletic scholarship.

"Oh," he said, "I dint take it after all. I quit, and I'm drivin' a truck now."

It was midsummer and he was wearing a long-sleeved shirt. "I can't never wear short sleeves agin," he said.

The idea of removals interests many tattoo artists, perhaps because of the possibilities of greater money-making. The idea fascinated me for a time and I made some investigational experiments.

In 1893 a St. Louis dermatologist, Dr. A. H. Ohmann-Dumesnil, advanced a method for tattoo removal; it was based on his observations of African primitives and their techniques for tattoo eradication. They first excoriated the flesh and then placed a fresh-cut African pawpaw flesh-side down against it. He reasoned that the active principle, a proteolytic enzyme, digested the color under the flesh and released it from its cellular bondage, allowing it to "float" to the surface as a scab, which could then be lifted off.

The preparation he used, a glycerole of papain, had been made in the early 1900s by a large pharmaceutical house, but a letter to their archives brought the response that the manufacture of this preparation had been stopped in 1910, when the formula had been sold to a smaller house—which had gone bankrupt in 1913.

I wrote again to the archivist, who then sent us the complete formula. But then our troubles started. In the five decades that had elapsed since the glycerole had been manufactured, over three hundred varieties of its basic enzyme had been made!

One can go just so far on a limited budget, and a limited number of persons who wanted a tattoo removed. We ran out of bucks and bodies. I finally managed to inject a drop or two of one solution made from one papain into a rose-leaf of a small tattoo on myself. Nothing happened for two weeks. I threw away my notes, as well as my record of which types of papain had been used—over sixty at that point.

And then the leaf started to dissolve! The skin in the small area of the leaf turned spongy and began to ooze a bit of serum. It frightened me into going to see a doctor who wanted to know just what the hell I had been doing to myself. I told him; he looked at me and shook his head sadly—told me to keep it dry . . . and pray.

In another month the crust came off, leaving no disturbance of the skin, no discoloration or scar—and the rose-leaf was completely gone! But I felt that any process which demanded three months' care was hardly practical as a working method, and the whole project was abandoned. I felt lucky to have escaped as I did, and could easily imagine the howls of impatient customers who would come knocking at the door if it were tried on them, suing me, and in general raising hell over such a prolonged treatment.

Thus vanished the dreams of get-rich-quick, and of the studio with two doors—one bearing the lettering "On," and the other the word "Off."

*   *   *   *   *

There are really only three or four "legendary" types of tattoos, but they are as much a part of the folklore of tattooing as the widespread idea that you can remove the designs with mother's milk.

The first is the idea of tattooing the penis like a barber-pole. Perhaps this has been tried, although I have never seen an example of it. But all the customers had! Four out of five persons, if the talk gets around to tattooed genitals, will swear that they have seen one. Just why a spiraling red line around the penile shaft should be so mysteriously attractive as an idea or an accomplishment is a great puzzle, perhaps connected subconsciously with the idea of "screwing" someone. Yet it remains the most often mentioned of all the erotic tattoos. Without doubt the shape of the organ would seem to lend itself to the application of a "barber-pole," but in execution it would be nothing except a ragged red line, whether the penis were tumesced or flaccid.

The second of the legendary tattoos is a "pack of hounds chasing a fox down across a person's back," with the fox disappearing into a convenient burrow. One practical question remains: how could you identify the fox if only his hind half showed? Perhaps you would merely place him in the nether region, just heading for the hole? At any rate, although thousands of persons have said they have seen such a tattoo, it is hardly reasonable that I should never have seen one in eighteen years and over a hundred thousand persons.

The third legendary tattoo is the fly on the glans, the head of the penis. I have seen such tattoos, but they are works of sorry success. The glans has a very different pore structure from the penile shaft which contains the corpus spongiosum. Attempts to tattoo the glans are met with such a gush of blood that the color is at once washed out. The remarkable quality of the flesh will not permit a hard and clear outline to be done; the results are thin and wavery, and hardly recognizable as flies. The glans is several times more sensitive than the shaft, which is comparatively insensitive when flaccid.

The last standard joke has always the same essence, although I have heard well over three thousand variants of the punch line. A man goes for a physical examination; the doctor notices a small black spot on his penis.

"What's that?" the medico demands.

"Aw doc," is the answer, "when it gets hard it spells out — " and here come the variations. In all the times the joke has been told, I have never heard the same punch-line twice. They ranged from "Winifred Witherspoon, Walla Walla, Washington" to "Sandy's Service Shop, Sandy Hook, New Jersey, to the very elegant French one: "Société Nationale des Chemins de Fer Françaises." The dot might double in diameter, but that's all, folks.

There is another small joke confined largely to sailors who would say: "I want a 'W' tattooed on each cheek of my ass and then when I bend over it'll spell 'W-O-W'." I got so tired of hearing this that I devised a counter to it. "Yes," I would add, "but if you stand on your head it'll spell something different." Many of the boys did not get it at all, and of those who did, some were offended.

The imaginations of the customers were wild things when it came to describing extraordinary designs. One example will suffice: "My buddy has the tattoo of a snake that begins with the head up biting his shoulder, runs down his back, wraps around his belly four [or five or six or ten] times, and then ends up with the tail on his ding-dong." I would generally deflate them by innocently asking: "How long did it take to have it done?" and get an answer something like: "It took two days" or "It took all evening."

Well, kids — such a design might well take six months to be applied if it were done in the size and width suggested. It is not possible to tattoo in any single area for more than a couple of hours. The continued prickings of the needles draw much blood to the region; the skin begins to harden and the colors go in with difficulty. There should then be a rest period for the healing; after that the skin in the area remains very sensitive. Moreover, many persons cannot endure the pain for long periods, and the tattoo artist wears himself out both physically and psychically. One of the things that keeps the tattooist happy is the continual change of clients — the arrival of fresh personalities to talk with and be investigated.

In a curious way the tattoo artist somewhat resents the client who already has an abundance of tattoos. Such persons feel that the tattooist should lower his rates for him; they feel that they are "special" customers. But the work remains the same for the tattooist. Many avoid such a situation with the well-tattooed customer by setting an hourly rate, and then working as fast or as slowly as they please.

*   *   *   *   *

The third category of misinformation applies to the care of the tattoo after it has been applied. For a period of about two weeks the design is in a very delicate condition. For the first two days the design remains bright and brilliant; then it begins to darken as the scab begins to form. By the end of a week the tattoo looks a mess.

This is the panic point, at which the customer feels his tattoo is not going to turn out well. He is tempted to pick at it — and when he does he picks out some of the color as well, so that even the best-applied tattoos seem speckled and faded. The scab should be kept intact and dry until it falls off without assistance. Anything done to hasten the healing process will result in the loss of from 30 to 50% of the coloring.

The young and impatient boot sailors found it hard to keep their hot little fingers off their new tattoos, or they'd heard from their shipmates that the quickest way to get rid of the scabs was to stand soaking them under a hot shower. And the result was always a faded old-looking tattoo.

The instruction card I gave out with every tattoo was very explicit after three re-writings, and couched in simple enough terms for everyone to understand if he could read. The text was:

1. Remove bandage in two hours. Then wash tattoo with soap and COLD WATER.
2. While tattoo is healing, do NOT apply vaseline or oily substances. Do NOT sunburn. Do NOT go swimming. Do NOT wash it.
3. Do NOT pick! Let scab fall off by itself. This takes about ten days.
4. The less you monkey with it, the better and brighter it will turn out.

Since most young people today find their attention wandering after two lines of print, it finally became necessary for me to tell them all these points verbally, as I was bandaging the tattoo. Still, they would go back to Great Lakes, where their older buddies would tell them to apply vaseline, wash it ten times a day, apply Noxema or shaving lotion. Admittedly it was difficult for the sailors to keep their arms dry while showering or passing a swimming test. All I could do was tell them to "favor the arm and keep it as dry as possible."

Once a young swabby burst into the shop. He had been tattooed three weeks before.

"Turned out fine," he said, pulling up his sleeve to show me the rose with "Mom" in the banner.

"Sure did," I said. "You must've taken good care of it."

"Oh, I did!" he said. "One of the older guys told me to rub fresh come on it, and I did."

"You *what*!?" I exploded.

"Sure," he said, grinning.

"Goddlemighty," I said. "Your own? Now I've heard everything."

The old idea of putting vaseline on new tattoos originated with the carnival tattoo artists. Year after year they made the circuit of the small towns and villages, and often they would find that during a stay in a town they had tattooed every available young man who wanted one. By telling the kids to keep the tattoo well-greased and washed frequently, they assured its loss of color. The following year the boy would probably ask to have it re-colored. "All right, but I'll have to charge you for it." Thus the worst jaggers were able to collect a few dollars even if they had no customers for new ones.

Unscrupulous tattoo artists like those in the syndicate shops in Chicago used to buy a bottle of Jergen's lotion and a box of empty half-ounce lead ointment tubes from a pharmaceutical house, have tiny labels printed with the words "Magic Tattoo Salve," fill each tube with the lotion and crimp the end, selling the tube for two dollars. The lotion faded the color, of course, although it did seem to promote faster healing. And then again there was an extra fee for re-coloring.

After the first crust of a tattoo comes off, there is a period of two to four weeks of "flaking." During this time the color is settling into the skin, losing its glossy surface, and at last taking on the matte finish of a completely healed tattoo. During the "flaking" period when small white scalings are evident, the healing can *then* be hastened by some sort of lanolin lotion, but no other substance should be used.

"There's no point," I used to tell the customer, "in paying out your money and then spoiling everything." The sensible ones agreed, but it was a continual struggle to get everyone to keep his hands off the tattoo.

"Play with yourself instead," I used to advise. "At least you can't do any damage to *that*!"

PART VI

The Clientele

GENERAL CONSIDERATIONS

Generalizations are dangerous to make — including that statement itself. Nonetheless, certain general comments may be advanced, without contradicting either logic or individual observations, about the characteristics of persons who get tattooed.

The most popular age for getting tattooed seems to be between eighteen and twenty. It is not that the boys do not want them earlier, when they first begin to feel that they are men; the laws in most states deny tattoos to anyone under eighteen. In the years when it was mandatory to carry draft cards, I always asked to see one. Even so, there were many times when I knew that boys had either borrowed draft cards or stolen them. They paid no attention to my posted notice that there was a federal fine of $10,000 and five years in the pokey for altering or exchanging draft cards.

Their ingenuity was often amusing. They wrote their own notes from mother until I had to make use of a notarized form to have her sign. Sometimes my suspicions were strong enough for me to telephone mother to see if she had really given permission to sonny — but underage customers elaborately dodged even that. If I called "home" I was sometimes answered by the thin reedy voice of a fifteen-year old girl, saying "Yes, I'm his mom, and yes, he can have a tattoo."

The fly-by-night jaggers in the syndicate arcades tattooed kids at any age, even down to thirteen, and the growing numbers of parental complaints to the mayor finally resulted in an Illinois law raising the minimum age of persons seeking tattoos to twenty-one. It was passed two years after the Illinois law allowing homosexual encounters with persons down to the age of eighteen. The syndicate jaggers complained loudly that young people could be permanently "marked" by such encounters, but were not permitted to be marked with a tattoo. "Which is worse?" the jaggers angrily demanded — but the falwells and the reagans won out.

The passage of the law destroyed a large percentage of the clientele in Illinois and shifted it to Wisconsin, especially Milwaukee. During the years from eighteen to twenty, the young man or sailor was yearning for his manhood initiation rite; after twenty, he wanted a tattoo for many other obscure or deeply buried reasons.

*   *   *   *   *

The years of tattooing gradually developed a curious sort of sixth sense in me that helped me determine — when a person came into the shop — whether he were actively interested in getting a tattoo, or merely browsing.

Certain signs helped me to see if he had what might be called a *general impulse to decorate*. If he wore a leather jacket there was always just a little too much on it in the way of embellishment — too many silver star-studs or fake jewels set in a pattern on the back of it, too many nailheads on his belt or around the heels of his motorcycle boots. His sideburns were always a little longer than usual, the hair "draped" in back, or "duck-assed" in the fashion of the mid-1950s.

Heterosexual males in those days could not generally wear ornaments, save for rings and tattoos; but after the beginning of the homosexual leather "movement," the decorations began to grow wilder and more numerous. Ear-rings appeared, but the impulse to get tattooed did not noticeably increase. It was impossible for me to analyze the reason for this from my necessarily superficial observings. Perhaps most of that early sadomasochistic crowd was phony, liking only the Fun & Games aspects of domination and submission, but not strongly enough to overcome the essential narcissism which kept the homosexual from "ruining" his body with tattoos.

Another general conclusion might be drawn from *the physical stance and attitude* of the customer. There was always a little too much swagger. Every movement was studied, a fact made much of by Jean Genet when writing about his criminal types in such novels as *Querelle de Brest*. When these young men stood looking at the flash their legs were always wide apart, feet firmly planted, thumbs hooked in the front or back pockets of their levis. When they took a drag on a cigarette — usually left dangling in the mouth — they tended to hold the cigarette exactly at the tip of forefinger and thumb, with the back of the hand up and the palm down, and elbow raised a little. It was very studied, imitative of the villains of the movies and TV shows in the 1950s. They were the presumed gestures of authority and/or violence, carefully executed in minutiae of details.

One boy, thickly decorated with a collection of ninety-six small two-dollar tattoos on his arms from wrists to shoulders, was Marty from Gary, Indiana. He was the most unbelievable pose-and-stance fellow of them all. The thumbs were always hooked in the broad belt or levis, the leather jacket always on, the speech coming from the corner of his mouth, full of "dese," "dose," and "dat," all delivered with eyes a-squint from cigarette smoke. He never turned; he pivoted on one heel and swung his body around, sometimes slow, sometimes fast. He was a tough, wiry, compact, and hairy young man — hard as a steel bar, or so he would have you believe. All this did not prevent him from getting woozy and nearly fainting when he got a fly on the topside of his penis. Marty was almost a caricature of what he tried to represent but within his limits he was one of the most faithful and amusing persons to come into the shop.

Another sign to look for was the old standby of military psychiatrists: *the fingernails*. Nails chewed or picked down to the quick was to them — in their necessarily hasty examinations of young draftees — always a sign of maladjustment, and a reason to probe more deeply. To me it was also a sign of young men and sailors who wanted tattoos, the "maladjustment" having led them already to this dread state of short fingernails from which a tattoodle might lift them back to love of country, Mom, and apple pie. But the falwells of the nation believed that a tattoo *caused* a boy to be bad and were unable to see that the tattoo might merely be a symbol of a condition that had already developed, possibly brought about by their own faulty rearing of the young.

One day while making change after a boy had paid for his tattoo, I dropped a quarter on the floor and he bent to pick it up. Finally he looked up at me, his face flushed. "Chee, Phil," he said, embarrassed. "I can't pick't up. I ain't got enough fingernails."

"You got any other serious problems?" I asked, ever the alert researcher.

"Well," he said, "I got this here real hankerin' after pussy. I jes' don't seem to get enough."

*   *   *   *

Perhaps ninety percent of the young men, the sailors and city boys who came in to get tattooed, belonged to the disadvantaged strata of American society. In America, where money or its lack is one of several determining factors about class, there is not the same dumb passivity of status acceptance that may be found in Britain. In the tattoo shops in America we can at least make the observation that the lower the class, the noisier and more belligerent the customer. This primary group, this ninety percent, had to be handled with a great deal of inventive diplomacy.

The remaining ten percent is difficult to classify or label in any way. It might include any or all classes. I have tattooed millionaires, bank presidents, the sons of wealthy Chicago families, presidents of corporations, movie stars and TV personalities, doctors and lawyers and a symphony conductor, novelists and journalists, judges and priests and policemen—in fact, the whole range of professions in all degrees of wealth and position. Admittedly some of the tattoos were very small, only token ones. The tattoo artist must be somewhat like a priest in the confessional, maintaining his client's incognito unless the customer has said he does not care. The subject matters and the motivations of the tattoos on the wealthy and high-placed have been fascinating, but they'll be carried into the dark place with me and not ever put on display.

Among white customers there was always a great curiosity about whether blacks could be tattooed, whether one could use the lighter colors—white, yellow, pink—on them. Unfortunately, the melanin layer on very dark-skinned blacks simply devoured the colors, none of which was intense enough to overcome it. Nor was there enough contrast between the pigments and the surrounding skin for the tattoo to be clearly visible. It was always necessary to tell very dark blacks this awkward truth—that the tattoo would not show up as well as it did on their honky acquaintances. Usually this might be done with some light remark about their "permanent tan." Some dark ones still insisted, however, and unaccountably seemed to be just as pleased with their nearly invisible tattoos as were their lighter-skinned friends. Sometimes I added a few white touches to an eagle's wing-tips or a panther's teeth, and the blacks seemed pleased with this extra concern.

Hardly any Orientals ever came into the shop. With the Japanese, who had carried the art of the tattoo to a high degree of perfection and complexity, a tattoo from a Westerner would be a little like carrying owls to Athens, coals to Newcastle, or transistor radios to Japan.

*   *   *   *   *

Most of the clientele was not very clean — except for the sailors, and often one had almost to scrub the skin surgically to make a clean place. Many of the customers really needed a bath. Often when a tattoo was being placed on the shoulder my fingers, tightening the skin from underneath, fell naturally into the bramble-patch of the young man's armpit, which very quickly became moist and even wet under the nervous tension of being tattooed. At first the odor of sweat was often noticeable, but when the great advertising campaign for deodorants began to take hold in America, the odors changed. They became dainty and violet-scented, or fragrant of lavender and other lady-like essences. I used to tease the boys a lot about their "dainty underarm odors," a phrase that made some of them squirm.

Occasionally a young man kept his money in his shoe, and bills from that source once in a while made life miserable. I finally followed a practice of taking shoe-money immediately to the back room and placing it in a closed box.

Drunks gave me a hard time, too. Although I did not object to a couple of drinks to give the customer courage, occasionally a real drunk slipped through my guard and the results were often disastrous, for drunks could never sit still. Their unexpected and sometimes violent movements often did irreparable damage to the tattoo. But in all the years of working on south State Street in Chicago I had to call on the police only once to handle a drunk.

Perhaps twenty or more sailors were in my shop on a busy Saturday afternoon when a very drunk street bum wandered through the door, peering around drunkenly and nearsightedly.

". . . wanna tattoo," he mumbled.

"Sorry," I said. I put down the needle and folded my arms, a trick used to direct the attention of everyone to the dialogue that was about to take place. "You've had too much to drink and you'll have to come back later when you're sober."

Usually that would be the end of it; the drunk would mutter something and leave. But this one stood swaying and insisting. Finally I said, "I'll have to call the cops if you don't leave." Still he stood.

I pressed the burglar-alarm bell which I had recently installed. It made a heluva racket right in the room, and the sailors jumped. The drunk still did not move but gazed around vacantly. I turned off the bell.

At that moment Sid, one of the two patrolmen on the beat, opened the door and came in. It astonished me as much as it did the others, because I am sure that the bell could not be heard on the street outside.

"Sid," I said, "we seem to be having a little trouble. There's someone here who's drunk and won't leave."

Sid was wearing sunglasses and the drunk was out of his line of vision, slightly behind him. Sid advanced on a tall swabby leaning against the case.

"What seems to be the trouble, friend?" Sid asked.

"No, not him," I said. "Behind you, Sid."

He turned and saw the drunk. I wished later that I had kept quiet. With the help of the swabbies I could certainly have evicted the drunk. But Sid went into action. He had a reputation on the street for his high-handed brutality in the treatment of bums. Now we all saw it at work.

He backhanded the bum across the mouth and then began to slap him around. Gradually a little blood appeared on the bum's mouth. Sid kneed him in the groin, and as he bent over Sid whacked him a couple more times. They waltzed around the shop, the sailors drawing back in a circle of horrified silence. Finally Sid took him by the collar and the seat of his pants and thrust him out the door, where he continued his mistreatment on the sidewalk. And then he signalled a passing patrol wagon, put the bum in, and came back into the shop.

"Got some kleenex?" he asked. I gave him some and he wiped his bloodied hands. I was shaking. "I'll put him in the can for vagrancy," Sid said. "Ninety days."

"Oh, Sid," I started to protest. "Not. . ."

"Teach him a lesson," Sid grinned nastily. "He just got out this morning after ninety days for drunkenness. Want to slap him with a charge of malicious mischief?"

I shook my head mutely and Sid left.

The sailors started to breathe again. "Jesus," one of them said, "I've often heard of police brutality—but that's the first time I ever saw it close up."

"Me too," I said, resolving at that moment never to ask for police help again.

One last observation might be made of the clientele in general. Certain persons feared the needle so much that they fainted after no more than a half-inch mark.was made of their skin. The number was about one in eleven.

After learning to recognize the symptoms of syncope I had a somewhat easier time with the "fainters." The signs were simple: a deep sigh, a cessation of talking, a film of perspiration on the forehead, preceded by a certain sidewise rotation of the head, or the hand at the back of the neck. The rush of blood away from the brain to the leg muscles to prepare the boy to make a dash from the place (all this on the subconscious level, of course) created a slight sensation noticeable in the main neck arteries. At the same time there was a cooling of the skin under my grip, and perhaps moisture appearing there. Finally the boy turned pale. Sometimes he asked for a glass of water for its purely psychological value—and interruption of the process—because it did nothing to help his dizziness.

At some point during these symptoms I would put away the needle and force his head down between his legs with a heavy pressure, telling him to press up hard against my hand. He would generally recover and after a moment we would resume.

But after this happened to one person it was bound to happen again soon. Fainting was contagious. If the room were full of waiting sailors, the next five or six would also become woozy. There was no way to avoid it. I grew to dislike the busy Saturdays when one sailor would faint, but there was no way to avoid the problem. The mysterious alchemy of shock in the body made many of the fainters want to defecate or vomit or at least get a drink of water. On the rare occasions when someone rolled off the chair in a dead faint without preliminary signs, more drastic measures had to be taken. Then I had to ask for help to pick him off the floor and put him on the slanted bench in the Trendelenberg position. Often the watching sailors asked why I did not finish the tattoo while the fainter was "out," but after seeing it happen to one, they no longer asked. The usual time for recovery was only fifteen to twenty seconds. The fainter came to after some convulsive movements and with a wild-eyed frightened expression and a "Where am I?" question. I would say "Hello! Have a good dream? You're in a tattoo shop getting a tattoo, and you fainted."

They often told me of the elaborate dreams they had in the brief fifteen seconds. Once, however, a boy was out for fifteen minutes. I later learned that he had a history of epilepsy. His buddies and I held him up by his feet, poured water on his face, slapped him, and all to no avail. He recovered just as I was about to phone for the paramedics and oxygen.

Part of the game, always played on a sailor about to get his first tattoo, was for his shipmates to try to scare him into fits ahead of time. They would tell him horrendous stories of the pain and the length of the needles, doing all they could to frighten him into fainting. Often they succeeded. Finally I began to tell the tormentors that if this boy fainted I'd charge them a dollar for every minute the tattoo was delayed. That had some deterrent effect, but not much.

Occasionally the boys who grew ill were really to be pitied. One Saturday afternoon a sailor waited about two hours for his tattoo. The watching and the remarks were too much for him. When his turn came he fainted without any warning signs. A Navy corpsman grabbed his head and tried to force it down between his legs.

"Too late for that," I said, and then noticed that the unconscious boy had lost control of his bladder, as often happens in syncope — that, or worse. The season was summer and he was in his whites. When he came around he was a sopping mess — pale, shaken, and utterly miserable. I put him on the slanted bench in the back room, thinking how unfortunate that his friends had seen it all and would thereafter tease him mercilessly for the rest of his days in boot camp. But there was nothing to be done. He stood shivering in front of the air-conditioner for a while, then put on his raincoat to hide the stain, and left to go back to the base—his very first liberty ruined.

Actually the pain of tattooing is not excessive—"no big thing," I would tell them—a kind of burning or extreme cold, as we have said before. It was totally unlike that of an injection by a doctor. "You don't feel the separate pricks," I used to say, and then after a timed pause—"Excuse the language . . . the pricks all run together and make the burning sensation." But subconscious fear—and *anticipando*—can do wonderful and terrible things to a person, as anyone involved in the Fun & Games of s/m will be happy to tell you.

THE LOVE AFFAIR
BETWEEN ARTIST AND CUSTOMER

One of the most mysterious and seductive enigmas in the tattooing business is the relationship that often develops between the tattooist and his customer, one that has been briefly mentioned before (see page 41). It is a quiet if rather intense sort of temporary camaraderie, brief-lived as a mayfly and perhaps rather shallow, which can be brought about when there is leisure enough to develop it.

Earl, the young gang-member with the extraordinary sideburns, used to drop in on quiet Sunday afternoons, sometimes for a small tattoo, and sometimes not. He had early established this curious kind of male bonding with me, and he continued it by talking about himself and his life, his triumphs and disappointments. His fine young face [what would it be like in twenty years?] with its ice-blue eyes and black hair and the long sideburns gave him the look of a young dandy of the 1890s. He was not well-educated and he shared all the usual prejudices of the lower middle-class, but he could talk intelligently of his hopes and dreams and plans. And the "love-affair" that developed between the young scoundrel and the old tattoo artist, the odd bonding, could only be explained by this curious phenomenon that was born during the first tattoo that I put on him.

A tape-recorder would have been the only way to reproduce the talk of the shop, but even that could not convey the *feel* of the place — the jests, the double meanings of the sexual talk, the gesturing, the fumbling, the hints of violence and purse-snatching and knifings, the thinly veiled and dimly-understood motivations of the herd-and-hero instincts. It was something you attempted to store away, remembering what you could and setting down some of it in the journal for Kinsey. Much of the talk was admittedly tiresome and repetitious, but each customer had his own air and attitude. Some of the things the boys said were outrageous, some hilarious, some revealing and poignant, and some just plain stupid. But put them all together and you had a view of life that could never be obtained in the ivied halls of the university.

I joshed them, scolded them, sympathized with them, and like a psychiatrist or scientist, never, never criticized. When one announced that he had just got out of the pokey, my response might be, "Whuffor you wanna be such a bad boy?" And once in a while one of them might look distressingly sad at that . . . The life that moved into and through my shop, always changing, was the real thing — there for me to see and touch and taste and enjoy after so many years of the unreal, the counterfeit, and the sheltered.

Why should the "love affairs" arise out of such ambience as this? For one thing, I tried to be nice to every one of them, tried to make each one feel that for the moment at least he was the most important person in the world. I had seen too many other tattooists be grumpy, curt, and short with their customers.

One evening there were six or seven sailors in the shop. We had been talking about everything and nothing in particular, when one of them suddenly said — as if he had made a momentous discovery: "Hey! You know, this is a lot more fun than goin' to a bar!"

The line of patter I used to help many of them over the rough spot, the strange and rather frightening experience of a first tattoo, was intended to put them at their ease.

"Are you nervous?" I would ask as the preparations began.

"A little," the boy might admit.

"Don't worry," I said. "Everyone is, no matter how many they get. Your first one?"

"Yeah."

"Ah!" I would say, busily shaving the hair off, sterilizing the area, applying vaseline to hold the thin coat of black powder that clung to the crevices of the stencil, "A virgin! I'm gonna get your cherry!"

A nervous laugh. "Well, maybe for *tattooing!*" he might say, even though I knew that half the fuzzy-chinned young boots from the small towns had never been closer to a girl than on the night of the high-school prom.

If they should be unlucky enough to get dizzy or faint, I would reassure them after they had recovered: "Don't worry. It happens to older and tougher guys too. I have a customer about forty years old and every time he comes into the shop he hollers, 'Hey Phil, get out the bench!' And do you know why? Because when I make a line on him a half-inch long—bang! he falls right out of the chair in a dead faint. So he has to have all his tattoos done lying down. Must have fifty on him."

They always felt a lot better after that.

All through the progress of a tattoo I would keep up a running line of chatter about the customer, where he was from, how he liked the Navy if he were a sailor—partly to keep his mind off the pain, and partly because—for the moment—I was genuinely interested in him. Many tattooists worked in surly silence, interested only in slapping on the design, getting the money, and making room for the next customer.

Sometimes I asked them how it felt, and would use their answers as an excuse to tell them: "A swabby was in here once and I asked him the same question. He cocked his head to the side, looked thoughtful for a moment and then said, 'Well, you know, it kinda reminds me of the time I peed into an electric fence.'"

It was wise not to have the needle working in the skin when that remark was made, because the customer's laugh would shake the rest of him.

Sometimes half-scolding, half-joking, I would upbraid them for their fears: "Aren't you a 100% red-blooded, snatch-lovin' American sailor? [Or soldier or marine.] You're supposed to be brave."

Often there came an honest response, something like that of the young man who said: "Not me—I'm the small, weak, and cowardly type."

After the tattoo had been washed and sterilized, a final swab of alcohol was applied as a last precaution. "Now," I'd say, "I have one final little treat in store for you." It stung quite a bit if the tattoo were large, and the customer might say "Ouch!" And then I would say, applying a liberal coating of carbolated vaseline before the final bandaging: "Well, we'll put on some purified babyshit and that will take the sting away." Occasionally I told them that the final vaseline was really glue and that I was pasting the tattoo on good and tight.

All this superficial running stream of nonsense went on continually, but deeper down something else was happening. A curious change would take place in the customer when the needle began to buzz. Perhaps he was surly or frightened at first, but suddenly he might relax and begin to unfold. I seemed to undergo a change in their eyes, a psychic alteration that made of me a more trusted counselor than any of their acquaintances or relatives. If the conditions were right, there would tumble forth from them details they had surely never told to any other living human being. It was almost as if the tattoo needles contained a truth serum instead of a pigment.

This freedom in talking, this unhindered revelation and trust was perhaps the single most astonishing thing noted during all the long years of tattooing. The explanation for this opening of the gates of self-revelation has always lain beyond me and perhaps always will. It did not resemble in any way the encounters between bartender and sobbing drunk, for there was no rationalizing in these uninhibited confessions. It was a strange and rewarding experience for me, and learning about my clients emotionally and intellectually was almost as gratifying as a roll in the hay. Yet sometimes I was left as jolted as they seemed to be cleansed and relieved. And now and then I treasured their confidences almost as much as the money collected for their tattoos . . .

. . . but not quite.

THE FLEET'S IN

Back in those days when tattooing still retained much of its mysterious quality for me, and even before putting on my first tattoo, the associations between tattooing and sailors were strong. My imagination always pictured an old grizzled salt with a rolling gait, his arms covered with the designs he had got as mementos of his visits to faraway places. But after I saw Kenneth Anger's art film *Fireworks*, the salts I pictured were not so grizzled nor so old, but young and handsome and tough. At no time, however, did the mystique surrounding the tattoo stretch so far as to include any swabbies who looked like Popeye.

It was quite a surprise and shock, therefore, when I saw the kind of sailors that came into my shop in Chicago. They were kids — quite young, eighteen — and some of them whose parents had signed consents for Navy service were only seventeen. Their chins were still peach-fuzzed, waiting for the first shave. They were pimply and gawky and adolescent, and full of big talk. For many of them, the boot-camp at Great Lakes Naval Training Station represented their first trip of more than a few miles from home. They had been yanked from the farms of the midwest, their heads shaved, their bodies clothed with ill-fitting uniforms; and had been set down among a crowd of similarly bewildered and frequently homesick boys. And then they had been taught a new language, in which they referred to the toilet as the "head," walls as "bulkheads," floors as "decks," and beds as "racks." They now spoke of swabbing the decks, of "liberty" as a pass to town; the top parts of their uniforms as "jumpers," and their workshoes as "boondockers." The small blue bags they carried were "AWOL" bags, pronounced "a-wall," and wastebaskets were "shitcans."

Sometimes at Great Lakes there were older sailors who had been at sea and had returned to attend a speciality school for additional training. One quickly learned to distinguish the boots from the "school-boys" for the older ones were closer to what the general idea of a sailor should be. They walked with a certain roll, and often wore the small white half-circle on the right shoulder of their jumpers that announced the name of their ship. Many of the sailors — both older and younger — preferred to spend their liberties in civilian clothes, thinking such clothes would enable them to pick up girls more easily — a wildly mistaken conviction. The older ones arranged to park their uniforms at a locker-club just outside the base and change to civvies for their trips to Chicago or Milwaukee. But one thing usually remained the same: their shoes, and by their feet I knew them. The military shoe could hardly be mistaken, nor could the short military haircuts be concealed. Their impersonations of civilians during their weekend liberties were hardly successful if you looked at shoes and hair.

With the young boots — in Chicago on a first liberty, and with a twenty-dollar bill in pocket — one had to adopt a somewhat paternalistic attitude. With the "school-boys" it was more a man-to-man approach. Each group had to be addressed in its own lingo. The boots wanted a lot for their "flying twenty"; out of it they expected to pay not only their rail-fare to Chicago and back, but to have a big steak dinner, get drunk, have a woman, and be tattooed. For ninety-five percent of them, the first liberty was a flop.

All in all, they were an amusing bunch, and they made up at least half of my business. There were not nearly as many Army or Marine customers as Navy, and the Air Force fly-boys at Chanute Field nearby were severely discouraged from getting tattooed at all. The popularity of tattoos among the armed forces was greatest in the Navy, with Army second, and Marines third. Far down the scale was the Air Force, with only a numerical sprinkling.

As time went on, I gradually grew weary of the sailors' big talk and endless repetitions, but tried to maintain a benevolent attitude and still make them feel important. But they slowly grew into a blur in my memory, with only a few of them memorable or outstanding. I did not often learn their names, but my memory for faces was good. There was one thing beyond me: recalling what design I had put on which one. Another block occurred when one came into the shop and said: "Say, you remember that guy I was in here with a coupla weeks ago . . ." When one saw between two and three thousand sailors a year, and when most of them said and did the same things, the ability to separate the actual events of a particular day dissolved completely.

But certain ones and certain events left vivid imprints and were noted in the Kinsey journal, and remembered with clarity.

There was the very timid small "gob-let" who came in alone one Saturday evening, shortly before it was time to take the special boot-train back to Great Lakes.

"Where can I buy a pair of girl's panties?" he said, blushing furiously.

"Whatsamatter?" I said. "You rip 'em off in your hurry?"

"N-no," he stammered, very confused. "It's just that all the guys kid me so much, I've gotta take sumpin back. For proof," he added.

There was one foam-rubber "falsie" in the shop, the largest cup size. To take the nervous customer's mind off his tattoo, I used to place the falsie on his knee and put his hand on it, telling him to close his eyes and think of something more pleasant than the tattoo.

"How about this?" I said. "You could make up all sorts of stories about this."

"Chee!" he said, delighted. "Could I have it? How much is it?"

"Nothing," I said. "On the house. All for the morale of the Navy."

The next week he came back and rather shyly presented me with an "official" Great Lakes cigarette lighter.

"How'd it go?" I asked.

"Jes' fine," he beamed. "They all think I'm the great lover."

Then there was the boot who got his nickname "Spotty" written on his left forearm. "How'd they ever come to call you that?" I asked. "From beatin' your meat and gettin' spots on your pants?" said I, hardly thinking it was so.

To my astonishment he turned pink, nodded, and giggled.

"That's just how I got it," he said, halfway proud.

Later when he came back for regular boot-camp (he had been a reservist), he still had the tattoo; he didn't want it covered. He thought it gave him a kind of air.

One hilarious Sunday I was busy putting a tattoo of a Navy Wave, a "first-class" with an enormous bosom, on the arm of a fat older sailor who had been in the Navy for seven years. Watching the process was an ex-Marine about thirty years old, and the two fell to talking. The usual chip-on-shoulder attitude of the two services was not evident, perhaps because the Marine had been out of the service for some time.

And what were they talking about? Babes, booze, and baseball? Not on your life. They were discussing techniques of parboiling and broiling, and how the cap'n liked little cookies with nuts on 'em and a maraschino cherry on top. Recipes! It turned out they were both cooks in the commissary branch of their services.

One hot afternoon two swabbies came in. One of them sank down on my three-legged stool and let out a groan. "Jesus," he said, "my feet hurt."

His buddy chimed in: "So do mine. We been walkin' around this town all day long."

"And haven't found anything?" They knew what I meant.

"I've got just the thing for you," I said. They looked expectant. I opened a drawer and rummaged in it, and came up with a card of Dr. Scholl's corn-pads. "Just what you need."

The first sailor grabbed them. "I'll say it is," he said. They both took off their shoes and socks and applied the corn-pads where it hurt the most. Then one sailor put his sock back on and wiggled his toes.

"Tell you what," he said with relief. "When you get right down to it, that's a lot better than findin' a woman."

I invested in an electric shoe-buffer for the shop and found it an immediate success. "Chee," a sailor said, "wisht we had one of these for the barracks. D'guys'd line up for it more'n chow."

It worked very well, provided that that the boys had a good basic spit-shine to begin with. On rainy days it was put away because it might fog their shoes or dirty the buffers with mud. One of the most amusing things about it was the position the sailors took to put the shoe underneath the buffer. Since their bell-bottoms were so long, every one of the guys grabbed the trouser legs, one at a time, and with a curious little feminine gesture like that of a girl holding up her skirt, would stand in such a position while getting the buffing. I would occasionally twit them with "Hold your skirt a little higher," at which most of them would let go of it entirely, somewhat embarrassed.

One evening a handsome older sailor came into the shop. He was tanned and healthy and with a certain amount of pride he wore a black eye from a street fight the night before. He swaggered over to the working-area and started to sit on the three-legged stool.

There was a ripping sound. He reached down under. "Jesus," he said, "I've split the canvas."

So I unfolded the screen and handed him needle and thread. He lowered his white pants quite unconcernedly, not taking them off, and started to sew them up. He was quite deft and I complimented him.

"I don't know about this here man's Navy," he grumbled as the needle flashed. "Seems to me it's more a woman's branch of the service. You're always washin' clothes or sewing buttons on or some damfool thing like that."

Once I bawled out a scared-looking little boot who was getting a Catholic cross on his arm, because he was squirming around too much. I was very stern about it and without realizing it I slipped back into my academic tone-of-authority. But I was jarred out of it when he said, looking very frightened and remorseful: "Yes, Father."

Occasionally a sailor would cross himself before I began, a gesture that always startled me.

Some sailors gave me doubts about literacy in the Navy. One Saturday a big rawboned boot sailor rattled off an obscene "toast" which his buddies thought very funny. I laughed too, said I had never heard anything like it, and asked if he would copy it off for me. It had sounded like an irregular pattern of alternating iambic trimeter and tetrameter with some feminine endings. [There — that'll prove that part of my heart is still in Academe . . .] The sailor screwed up his face, took a pencil, and with the tip of his tongue protruding from the corner of his lips, produced the following copy, which those who care may try to decipher:

May your Bleeding Bowls distres you may corn
addor your feet may crabs as big as hors tirds
craw apon your ball and eat and wen your ole and febel
and a sisaphalic reck may your spin drop thro yor
ashole and brake yor Fucken neck.

At other times I was astounded. Some of the Navy personnel were really quite intelligent, and now and then a match for whatever degree of sophistication I possessed. One sailor looked at me narrowly after listening to me talk for a while, and announced flatly: "You haven't always been a tattoo artist. I think you may have been a university professor."

His observation jolted me considerably, but since we were alone in the shop I confessed that he was right. I asked him not to say anything about it, lest he frighten away the others. Many Navy boys showed surprising degrees of education and background; these were not the ones, however, who generally got tattooed.

Now and then my "sophistication" could hardly cope with their directness and simplicity. One sailor, quite drunk, listened for a while one evening and then suddenly came over to me and clasped his arm around my neck.

"Do you like sailors?" he demanded. The others looked on curiously.

"Sure I do," I said. "I've seen a lot of you here in the shop."

"Well, I'm glad," he said, "because I sure as hell like you." For one awful moment I thought he was going to kiss me, but he didn't, and all the others laughed.

The lack of sophistication in these midwestern farm boys made them particularly vulnerable to the tricks and gimmicks of the conmen of the big city. They were easy victims not only of devices used by the Pacific Garden Mission but of the unscrupulous photographers who offered them a "free" photograph—but then sent the rest of the order C.O.D. to mother back on the farm, separating her from at least twenty-five dollars.

One of the more obnoxious scams practiced on the street was called the "Murphy gag," perhaps originated by a man of that name. South State Street was always full of pimps, real and pretended. The phony ones picked on the boot sailors, promising to produce girls for them. They fast-talked ten bucks out of the swabby, then led him to a dark stairwell, and told him the girl was behind the second door on the left. When the sailor knocked he found either an empty room or an irate husband. Meanwhile, the pretended pimp had made off with the money.

I was explaining this trick to a group of sailors when one of them piped up to say, "Gee, thank you, sir; no one ever bothered to tell us that before," and there was a small chorus of "Yeah," and "Thanks."

On summer weekends the sailors flocked into my shop in such numbers that it was necessary to begin a policy of "Navy first," requesting the city-boys to come back later, or on another day. This brought me the ill-will of some of the town-boys, and was a rather high-handed discriminatory tactic, but it was managed without too much offense.

Much of the talk in the shop was nothing but gossip and bullshit, and many topics came up for brief or extended discussion. One day we were turning over the matter of parental reaction to tattoos, and suddenly one sailor spoke up to say that *his* parents would not complain.
"How so?" I asked, ever the universal straight man.
"Well," he said, "my father was a Seabee working in Cuba and he got killed, and my mother committed suicide when she heard the news, so they won't object." That was a conversation-stopper, all right, and for several minutes there was no further talk in the shop.

On a day in mid-July a hot and dusty-looking swabby came into the shop with his Awol bag.
"Where you from?" I asked, and he said Bainbridge, Maryland. It seemed that he was about to go into Naval Air Reserve Officers' Training School, and that part of the examination was an interview with a psychiatrist, who asked if he had any tattoos. The boy said yes, two—an anchor on his arm, and one on his butt that he had got in Houston. The one on his behind was the same slogan that was sometimes seen on automobile rear-bumpers: "If you can read this, you're too damned close."
The psychiatrist had blown his top, classified the tattoo as "indecent and obscene," and told him that if he wanted reserve officers' training he would have to have it removed or covered. The poor swabby had looked all around Bainbridge and the east coast, but couldn't find anyone to cover it, because all the tattoo artists had "exposed" shops and could not do such private work.
So he had hitch-hiked all the way to Chicago to get me to do it, for he remembered that my shop was not "exposed" to the street. I

put some flowers and leaves over the words, wondering what kind of complexes the shrink himself was battling. In the old days such a statement on a boy's ass would have been good for a laugh, not a Freudian interpretation of . . . what? In a kind of oblique sense the Navy seemed bent on "abnormalizing" the boys: it would not let them have pin-ups in their lockers, took away from them at the main gate any match-book covers that had pictures of girls on them, and discharged them if they were caught masturbating. Then it threw them with their overly-hot-eighteen-year-old blood into an exclusively male society for several weeks as boots.

On another occasion a little boot bounced into the shop and said excitedly: "Chee, dis is Sparrow's! Dat's all we talk about inna barracks — dat amusement park called Riverview and Sparrow's! More of your cards are bein' swapped around the barracks than liberty cards!"

One of the items of decor in my shop was a genuine human skull that I had picked up somewhere. I filed a slit in the skullpan and stuck a German dress dagger through it, balancing the whole on the dagger-point, and stuck some artificial roses into the eye-sockets to make it a reasonable copy of several tattoo designs on the "Death Before Dishonor" motif. It created quite a lot of comment. One remark was made by a sailor from Georgia.

He looked at it and said, "My daddy's got one of them. It's a nigger's. He keeps it on the mantelpiece." And then since no one — including myself — said anything, he went on: "Well, you know, we live kinda hard down South. He shot him hisself."

At which I said, "And did he go to jail for it?"

The swabby let out a short harsh laugh. "Are you kiddin'?" he said. "In the South?"

When it came his turn to get tattooed — a rebel flag — oddly enough he fainted three times. No one seemed to understand why. After I finished with him — and before the next customer — I turned the rheostat back down to its regular setting, and shortened the needles so that they did not extend more than their usual length from the end of the tube. The next customer was not troubled with getting woozy. After the Georgia boy had left, pale and shaken, an observant older sailor said, "Mr. Sparrow, I think you are an instrument of justice."

One sailor, a nice friendly curly-haired guy, came in to get a fairly large geisha girl on his leg. He pulled a piece of crumpled paper from his pocket and asked me to put the Japanese characters under the figure. "It's my girl's name in Japanese," he explained.

"Ah, Lieutenant Pinkerton," I murmured, thinking of *Madame Butterfly*.

He looked blank, so I explained. Then he said, "When we had to leave each other she suggested that we commit suicide together. But I thought I might be too young for that. I'm gonna try to get back to her. I'm workin' on a transfer."

"Yet shee / Will be / False ere I come / With two or three," I said, quoting Donne. "Be careful you don't get the Japanese rot," I said, half-jokingly.

"I think I already got it," he said, "on my dong."

"Well, be sure not to give it to Miss Cho-Cho-San, your cherryblossom."

"Hell," he said, "I think that's mebbe where I got it in the first place."

Ah, the Navy!

By far the saddest group to come into my shop — and they came in large numbers — were the rejects, those who did not quite make it into the Navy even though they had passed their draft-board physicals. Perhaps something was wrong physically, perhaps personality-wise, which came to light during the more rigorous examinations at Great Lakes. Since on arrival at the base they had sent their civilian clothes home, and because they had not been sailors long enough to be allowed to wear the uniform off the base, the Navy furnished them with a "going-away" uniform. This was a pair of dark slacks, a maroon or black or brown corduroy jacket, and an absurd little tweed hat with an Alpine feather on it. This ensemble made them easy to recognize, and they all carried a large manila envelope with their papers.

One of my many standard questions was whether they were happy or sad to be out. The majority regretted it, and the tattoos they got were always Navy ones, a kind of face-saving gesture, perhaps, to help protect them against the talk back home. Sometimes the answers were flippant: "Oh, the Navy's a great life—you can't beat it!" said one, and waited twinkling until I reacted to his pun about masturbation.

One of them, alone on a rainy night in the shop, broke down and cried. "I jus' can't go back home," he sobbed. "My father was a twenty-year man in the Navy, and my brother's been in twelve."

At eighteen one cannot be comforted over such a tragedy, nor know that his "disgrace" will be forgotten after a year. There were other tales of obesity and broken ear-drums and flat feet and bone-disease and rheumatic fever, and there were a few who said more or less shamefacedly that they just didn't fit into the Navy. It took a lot of consoling to help some of them over this difficult moment.

On the pleasanter side—one thing was very flattering. A whole company—approximately eighty-eight boys—decided that every one of them would get a tattoo from me. Not all of them got the same tattoo, of course, but they divided themselves alphabetically in the barracks, and then came in on four successive Saturdays, filling the days full, for I never worked fast enough to do more than about twenty-three tattoos a day. The item made the newspapers.

After leaving Chicago and spending a year of weekends in Milwaukee, I never saw the boots again. California had an entirely different breed of sailors. They had all been to sea, and the initial period of thinking had passed, that "a sailor's not a sailor until he's been tattooed." All of the Oakland sailors were seasoned old-salts, wearing their shoulder patches for the USS Hancock, or the Coral Sea or the Enterprise or Midway or other ships of the line.

I missed the boots. I missed their youth and freshness and naivete and big talk. They were a rewarding refreshment that I will long remember.

CITY-BOYS, EX-CONS, AND JUVENILE DELINQUENTS

Many years of dealing with city-boys, gang-members, ex-convicts, and similar individuals helped to evolve a theory about such customers, one calculated to raise hackles on the necks of most sociologists and psychologists.

There is a war on, an unending battle between the generations. It grows more intense year by year. There is much supposition and argument about the causes of juvenile delinquency and its appearance in more matured forms in such older groups as the Hells Angels. All of the theorizing smells of the oil of scholarship, and the usual litany of reasons like "broken homes" and "early childhood traumas."

Not only has the battle been joined, but there is another important facet in the thinking of the "bad" ones, and that is: "Yeah, the war's on, but where are the reporters to give us the publicity?"

A tattoo for the gang members or the delinquents was the visible sign of their rebellion, their manliness, or their affiliation with the stratum that was in revolt. To know this crowd one had to be one of them, to pretend to scorn the "fuzz" the way they did, to accept their motives without criticism, and never to be shocked at anything one heard—in other words, to be an "older delinquent." For them I performed a function of which their parents disapproved (that is, of which the "enemy" disapproved) and I was therefore one of them. My trick succeeded. They talked freely in front of me.

My literary background had made me familiar with the stories of King Arthur and his knights and the literature of chivalry in the long dull poems of the fifteenth and sixteenth centuries. I knew of the exploits and customs of the Knights Templars and the Crusaders, and the exploits of the Red Cross Knight and others in Spenser's *Faerie Queene*.

As time went by a dim suspicion began to shape itself in my mind, which finally took this form: the juvenile delinquents of the present day were conforming almost exactly to the chivalric code. There was the ritual search for members who—once found—had to undergo the ritual probation and initiation. Then there followed the ritual sortie, the trial period when the new member went out to prove himself, either in search for the Holy Grail or overcoming the infidel or the paynim—or today's enemy, the adult. The fact that delinquents proved their mettle by burglary, "rumbles" or fights, vandalism, drinking large amounts of liquor quickly, theft, violence, sexual exploits or even murder did not essentially set them apart from the knights, save in the nature of their goals. Their procedures were the same.

The adult world had lost the allegiance of the delinquents. Adult life was tiresome, boring, repetitious to the young. It was inert; they were alive. They were parasitic upon it, yes, but they wanted no part of it. It represented *Sloth* or *Idlenesse* in Spenser's terms, and idleness was a kind of death for the young.

In addition, the young ones saw with appalling clarity the hypocrisy of the adults — how the old ones insisted always upon the young following a set of rules, laws, and precepts which they themselves continually evaded or shattered in their own lives and activities. A hatred for the adults grew large in the juveniles. One boy once said to me, clenching his fists in a very real physical hatred, "It's all I can do sometimes to keep from knockin' the hell outa my old man, 'specially when he gets off on one of his lectures about how I should do, when he's done just the opposite the day before."

The adult community through its increasing inertia has permitted the growth of the juvenile gangs and allowed them to penetrate the adult grouping, and even sometimes to gain control of it by the kind of dynamism which is to be found in the adolescent. The young form themselves into a social unit, frequently autocratic, often monarchical, but always more *alive* than the adult community. By adult standards their aims may be considered perverted, but they nonetheless have within their limits a sense of duty and honor, loyalty and co-operation, heroism and sacrifice, industry and planning and accomplishment; and a system of rewards, penalties, punishments which puts the adult community to shame. Their activities — which seem to the adult unprovoked and senseless — have, for themselves, very real meaning. And the punishment which always threatens the existence of the young, hanging over them like the Damoclean sword, never succeeds — and never will — in restraining them or correcting their behavior to follow the adult "norm." It merely alienates them, drives their allegiance farther away from the adult world, and increases their fealty to their own gang members.

So — the war is on. One day a young gang-member burst into the shop, highly excited. "We got our pitchers in the papers!" he said. [Witnesses and reporters of the war . . .]

"Where?" I asked.

"In the *Daily News*," he said. He pulled a clipping from his pocket. "Here!"

The newspaper photo was of a car half-sunk in the Des Plaines river, its back wheels resting on the bank. "Where are you?" I said, puzzled.

"Oh, we're not there," he said loftily. "But it was our gang done it."

The newspapers and TV reporters by taking notice of the gang exploits furnish them with the second most powerful motivation for their activities, that of public notice and witnesses. The kids doted on publicity. The longer and more detailed the news treatments, the more carefully and elaborately they planned the next rumble, escapade, or sortie. They had to live up to their dynamic reputation.

It did not take long to recognize the type of the delinquent—the gnawed and bitten fingernails, the sideburns, the levis or black pants or chinos (as the fashions changed) peg-topped or hanging very low around the hips, the duck's-ass haircuts (or the ragged types, of which there were about six in the 1950s), and all the other outward signs which were the indexes to them. Such signals rarely failed. And the minds the boys revealed were often curiously troubled, uncertain and yet hiding the insecurity under bravado, a quality that increased in direct ratio to the number of friends accompanying them in a group. Often such insecurity masked itself as arrogance or brutishness.

Perhaps one cause of their problems was that civilization was forcing everyone to rotate in a smaller circle, diminishing the area of loyalty. These young delinquents illustrated this idea perfectly. Boys and men—from the Greeks onward—have always grouped in gangs or clubs; and so have today's adults in their Kiwanis, Rotary, Lions, or Masonic organizations. But the distinction between the gang members ["we"] and the outsiders [the adults, "they"] seemed particularly sharp in the 1950s and 1960s—and perhaps at the present time of the 1990s.

Among themselves, the young held to all the cardinal virtues of the adult world—without the hypocrisy, however. They were—and continued to be—faithful to each other; but they were so conscious of their separation from the mainstream that they felt that nothing beyond the gang limits was worthy of their loyalty or allegiance.

And—conformity again—when one got a tattoo, they all wanted one.

Another odd observation—gathered from much eavesdropping—was that there was always one guy in every wolfpack who was "taking care" of the others. At first I did not know what the phrase meant, but it finally became obvious that "taking care" had a sexual meaning. Ken was the one in the Road Wolves. By listening to the others describe him when he was absent, and with a little deduction, I learned the truth. The unusual thing was that to the other gang members who were pleasuring themselves from all of Ken's apertures he was not "queer," but "just one of our buddies who is fixin' us up." They protected him from outsiders but at the same time they kidded him unmercifully about being queer.

Even as close as I came to the charmed circle of the Road Wolves, mine was still a fringe existence; I was wholly trusted by them but never quite a part of them. Of course, I never asked to be. Similarly, social workers who infiltrated the gangs and pretended to wink at the law in order to be one of them, might superficially succeed but never deeply nor completely.

"You know, Sparrow," one of the Road Wolves said to me once, "we're thinkin' of makin' you an honorary member."

"Nothing would please me more," I said.

"Of course, you'd have to pass the initiation," he said, twinkling.

"Is it hard?" I said.

"You'd never be the same again," he said.

Luckily he forgot about it.

They talked a lot about homosexuality and about how they beat up "the goddamned queers" after they jackrolled them. Several times, with different gangs I even dared go so far as tell them what "the psychologists said": that they were fighting the same thing in themselves when they bashed gay persons. No one ever took a poke at me for saying such a thing, largely because it was said with a smile and at the proper psychological moment, with a kind of twitting attitude. Perhaps they didn't swing on me because they did not quite understand what I was saying.

The fact that I seemed to be on their side and was able to furnish them with their "badges" opened most of the gangs to me, but I failed with the "Vice Lords," the most tightly knit, belligerent, and notorious of all the Chicago gangs in the 1950s — notorious because the newspapers took greatest notice of them and by so doing encouraged them to go farther.

One member of the gang called the "Rebels," a fellow named Andy, came in to get his tattoo because he had been a leader of a group of his buddies who had roughed up two cops in a bowling alley. He got the rebel flag with his name beneath it, and thereupon became a "senior" member in his gang's hierarchy, entitled to wear the flag as a symbol of a violent encounter with the police.

But not all of their sorties were successful. Sometimes the kids got caught, like Gordon, whose particular task was to steal a car. He had tried several times and had not been able to do it. Gordon was a big young man about six-two, with carefully coiffed brown hair above a good face that looked like that of a page-boy of the Renaissance. He spent many hours in the shop. I had locked the two drawers of a filing cabinet with a pair of handcuffs; he was always wanting to try them on to see if he could escape their clutches. From him I learned the trick of clipping off one end of a girl's bobby-pin and using the thin metal strip to slide down over the ratchet in the handcuff lock so that it would open easily.

"Dillinger always wore a bobby-pin down there in his hair," he said, pointing to his crotch, "so's if he got caught by the fuzz he stood a chance of breakin' away."

Gordon wore one "down there" too, but he couldn't ever seem to get at it to free himself from the handcuffs, although he practiced over and over. He was finally arrested for car theft; he had been caught, and was presumably in bad odor with his gang, the "Valiants." For a time they considered the penalty of making him have his gang tattoo covered, but they finally decided to be merciful.

Little Glenn of the "Road Wolves" was another gang failure. His last appearance in the shop was the most interesting. Gone was the duck's-ass haircut; he was in a suit and very quiet. He asked to have the wolf-symbol of his gang covered, and then told me the story.

He had been to Mexico with Herb, another member. Together the two, working without the monarchical sanction of the leader, had found $4,000 in an open private garage as they were walking down an alley trying to steal some tools.

"The guy must've been tryin' to hide th' money from his wife. Anyways, Herb and me found it stashed inna box, all fifties and twenties, and we took off for Mexico. And when we got back we was caught."

"How come?" I asked.

"Spent too much too fast," he said wryly. "And my ole man caught on."

"He turn you in?"

"Yeah," Glenn said, looking mad and murderous. "I'd like to kill th' sonofabitch," he said. "Mebbe some day I will, too, by God."

"Now, now," I said.

"Yeah? Well, he's got a radio and TV repair shop and he puts in parts you don't need when he gets a set to fix and then charges double what it's worth, and what's the difference I'd like to know between doin' what I did and what he does alla time?"

I had no answer for him.

Then there was Tony. I never did learn the name of his gang. He specialized in purse-snatching. "You know how to do it?" he asked. "You hit a woman from behind on the shoulder, opposite the arm she's carryin' the purse on, and nen you snatch it and slap her hard on the face, and man, she's too damned surprised and froze to holler or run."

"And so you get away before she gets un-paralyzed?"

"Yeah."

But about a month after his graphic description there was a small newspaper item about his getting caught for purse-snatching. Evidently some woman was not "froze" enough to keep from hollering. He had confessed to about forty snatchings, been identified by about twenty of his victims, and given two to ten in the pokey.

One of the most bizarre cases of the youthful gang-mind at work was that of Jimmy, whose father was a Chicago police sergeant. I had tattooed him twice, high on the shoulder, "so's my old man won't see it." One design was an Irish shamrock with "Erin Go Bragh" beneath it—very fitting, for Jimmy's face was like a map of

Ireland. He belonged—unknown to his father—to a gang called the "Dolts" [couldn't they have found another name?], but that group was too small to suit him.

He wanted a bigger "gang," and so—falling for the Hollywoodenized glamor of several movies then current, he joined the man-sized gang of the Marines and went to boot-camp at Pendleton in California.

He had not been gone long enough to "graduate" when he was back, looking a little shifty and hesitant. I asked him why. He said that he had an emergency leave because his aunt was ill, but it did not take him long to confess that he was AWOL from Pendleton, for the second time in two months.

He was a crazy mixed-up kid, his case symbolizing the difficulties of a whole generation of young rebels without a cause. Jimmy said his commanding officer was out to get him, and there was small wonder. Even more than in the adult world which he hated so much, he found in the Marine Corps the sort of boredom and discipline and hard routine which he loathed. He got six weeks in the brig the second time.

But it was the first AWOL that he talked about. He and Fred, another of the Dolts whom I had tattooed, had both joined the Corps together.

"Then we went AWOL when we couldn't take it any longer," Jimmy said. "Fred and me skipped out to Mexico City and spent all our money. And nen when we hadn't got no more we turned our selfs inta the American Embassy."

"Good thing," I said. "Probably made it go easier with you."

"But before that," Jimmy said, and his eyes were glittering, "right after our money was all gone, Fred said we should rob a gun store. So I ast him why and he said 'So we can get guns and make a last stand in a hotel room and shoot it out when they come for us. Or' he said, 'we can at least kill our selfs if it's hopeless.'"

"Jay-sus," I said.

"Yeah, we wuz serious," he said, and I believed him.

"Jimmy," I said, "what you were looking for in the Marines was the same sort of glamor and excitement you found in your gang activities. But you're never gonna find it. It always belongs to the other person in the next county, the other thing, the other situation.''

"Damn," he said, "they didn't notice me at all."

"Why do you want to be noticed?" I said, "What have you got to make anyone notice you? So far you haven't got much. No education—you dropped out of high-school. No skills, no talent—nothing in your life except this one plan for violence, and that didn't come off."

His eyes lighted again. "Boy, if it would've!" he said. "Then we'd have shown 'em!"

"Shown 'em what?"

He didn't know.

I was sorry for him but there was nothing I could do. His father was a strict disciplinarian but no psychologist, and the boy's ego had been badly battered. For my own protection, however, I could not have an AWOL Marine hanging around the shop. I told him that the Armed Forces Police often dropped into the shop to check IDs [they actually did] and that got rid of him in a hurry. He was too far gone in dreams and confusion for anyone except a trained psychiatrist to help him.

Another young man who had an even more spectacular career was Charlie, who was inclined to be a loner rather than a gang-member. I followed his downward path with the fascination of an observer absolutely powerless to intervene. Charlie had a job with Barnum and Bailey's circus, which came to town one summer, and when it left, Charlie skipped out of the job and stayed in Chicago. He was a young Italian from New York City, afflicted with a kind of impatience, wanderlust, and uncertainty about goals and aims which in some ways brought him close to the gang-members, but in others set him apart.

Charlie already had several tattoos. He made himself indispensable to me—or so he believed—by becoming an errand boy and handyman around the shop for no other payment than a free tattoo when the urge descended on him.

It did not take him long to become one of the wildest young men in Chicago. He was already smoking pot; it was only a step to bennies and goofballs, hustling the queers and jackrolling the girls he went with. He was high most of the time, especially after he found out the effects of bennies and barbiturates. After about a year he felt that he had had enough of Chicago; he would go back to his New York gang. He decided this after having his best suit stolen by a buddy he had been living with, getting his chest nicked with a knife wielded by a drunken Puerto Rican, and finally having his trench-coat sliced from collar to midriff in a fight with another drunk. When he began to case my joint in the questions he asked about locks and alarms, I gave him the few bucks he needed to make up what he lacked in bus fare to New York, thinking that perhaps I had got off easy.

Then he disappeared for six months, and I presumed he was in New York. But word reached me from a "classmate" of his that he had been arrested in the Greyhound Bus Station after still another fight with a "colored stud," and had been sent to the Vandalia prison farm.

When he showed up again he was full of large tales about wolves and pogeys (active and passive partners) in the "reformatory," and he was careful to insist that his time on the "farm" did not technically make him an ex-con.

"What the hell," I said, "no ordinary person would know the difference. And certainly not the newspapers."

"Just the same," he said.

He had been out only a day or two when he was back at his old pleasures even more enthusiastically than before. He was rolling his "gurls," smoking more marijuana than ever, and casing several apartments of the gays who picked him up, so that he could burglarize them later.

Then I was gone for a while in Europe, to see Alice Toklas and Jacques Delarue, an inspector of the Sûreté, who had written a book about tattooing in the French underworld.

When I returned, Charlie was in full swing. This time there was a wild tale about a hassle he had with two broads in a hotel room where he had set fire to a mattress, dumped one of the girls into a full bathtub with her clothes on, and then escaped the cops by diving from a third-floor window into a snowbank. He came to the shop with a Brooks' Brothers suit draped over his arm, four other suits, assorted cufflinks, a transistor radio and some other loot, all of which he had stolen from a swank Astor Street apartment. He gave me an explicit account of how he had got in, saying also that in the time I had been gone he had stolen and fenced a half-dozen portable TV sets, a set of silver with the initials "J.O.P." and many other things.

But the end came soon. He was caught and arrested, identified by many of his victims, given ten to twenty, and not seen after that.

A large young man whom I had once tattooed came back one day and saw the skull-dagger-and-roses arrangement on the work table.

"Gee, Phil," he said, "I almost got you a new skull the other day."

I was startled. "Where would you have a chance to get that?"

He looked sly. "Won't tell," he said, but I finally got it out of him. He had been working in a cemetery where they were moving old graves to new locations. His shovel had knocked a hole in an ancient wood coffin and the contents spilled out. "The bones was always fallin' out," he said.

"I'll give you any tattoo in the shop for one," I said.

He shook his head. "My tattoodlin' days are over."

"How's about twenty bucks for one then?" I said.

His face lit up.

"I'll try," he said. And then warming to his subject he told how they had a kind of hockey game one afternoon in the cemetery, using shin and thigh bones to knock a skull between the headstones, and how later the game had turned into what he called a "bone fight" with his picking up a thigh bone and beating his buddy over the head with it.

I shuddered. "Lord," I said, "how grisly."

"Naw," he said, "all the gristle was offn 'em by then."

It was this same boy who much earlier had said that he'd like to have something sentimental on his arm, and how about a pitcher of a man screwin' a woman, with "Mom" and "Dad" underneath it, huh?

The tattoos which were self-applied in prison were extremely crude. The amateur did not know enough to keep the skin taut, and the result was a series of black dots. The conception may have been grand, but the execution was poor—rough and primitive outlines, and of course no coloring except the black of soot from the ceiling or from burned toilet paper.

One evening a wolfpack of youngsters came to the shop. One of them had just been released from the pokey. "Chee, Sparrow!" he announced in a loud voice, "you're gettin' to be real well *known*! About half the guys in the pokey's got tattoos by you!"

I wasn't sure if I were more embarrassed or flattered.

A fellow with prison pallor came into the shop. He wore a railroader's cap and called himself Lucky. The tattoos on his hands and biceps were very crude; he said that he had got them in jail in Texas. He wanted some color added to a crude tombstone, with his mother's birth and death dates too, to join her name which was already there.

Another young man, also with a tell-tale pallor, wanted all of his half-dozen pokey tattoos covered because they reminded him too painfully of his jail term of eighteen months for car theft.

An unusual ex-con with the usual pallor beneath a heavy beard stubble asked to have a small black silhouette of a hand—fingers extended—put on the web between thumb and forefinger. Since he already had many pokey tattoos visible on his hands, I said yes.

"How much?" he inquired.

With my x-ray eyes I estimated the amount of money he had in his pocket. "A dollar," I said.

He shook his head. "I ain't got that much now," he said, "but I'll be back."

He did come back, two days later. This time he was shaved and smelled of after-shave lotion. He wore an Ivy League suit. I would not have recognized him save for his tattooed hands.

"Put 'er on," he said, and I did.

Midway I said: "I thought the Cosa Nostra or the Mafia was sort of particular about just anybody wearing a black hand."

He shrugged. "How do you know I ain't?"

When I finished he asked the price. I stuck to the original quotation of a dollar. He pulled a huge roll of fifties and twenties from his pocket and gave me a ten. I considered his progress from rags to riches pretty good for two days' time. I never knew whether he had mugged someone or robbed a currency exchange. Perhaps he had done both.

One young man came in with a creditable pokey job which he wanted colored in. It was a vine of well-done roses climbing up his arm. "I wouldn't want 'em covered up for anything."

A little conversation revealed that his name was Dewey and that he had heard about my work while in jail.

"Who put the roses on you?" I asked.

"Charlie."

"The runaway from Barnum and Bailey's circus?" I asked. "The wild kid I tattooed?"

"Yup," he said.

"Why wouldn't you want them covered?"

Dewey turned scarlet and stammered, "I-I g-guess they mean too much to me," he said.

And I knew why. Dewey was the farm-boy whom Charlie had "broken in" to be his pogey while they were in prison together, the "hot hole" that Charlie had mentioned. Echoes of Mr. Charlie kept reaching me for several years after he had eventually got out of prison and back to New York.

None of the ex-cons was particularly interesting, save that they represented a sampling and mixture of motivations. Many times — even before the wild explosion of drugs in America — I was asked to cover the "tracks" of a junkie, the damaged, raised, and blackened veins where he had taken his fixes in the "main line" of the arm at the elbow bend. I always refused, largely because the area was too bloody to work in and the pain too great. Besides, many of them had no other tattoos on the body, and one in the elbow bend would have been just as much a signpost of addiction to the police as the tracks themselves.

It may be somewhat cynical to include in this category of law-breakers the mention of "bad cops." There were several of these, and two brothers — who had Greek names — gave me one of the worst frights I had in years of tattoodling.

The incident occurred while I was still in the old arcade. Late one winter night they came in — Gus, the older tougher-looking one — and his brother Alex. I had been about to leave for the night.

"Hey, we want a tattoodle!" they yelled at me. They were both drunk and not in uniform.

"Come back tomorrow," I said.

"Not on your life," said Gus. "When we want a tattoo we want it." He looked down at me. "You ain't gonna say no to a coupla policemen now, are you, specially when they're brothers?"

"Oh no," I said. "Sit down. What do you want?"

They picked out two small designs. They were four dollars each. "How's about givin' us the two for four?" said Alex, staggering.

What could you do? Above all else, I didn't want the police against me. "All right," I said.

Gus suddenly drew his service revolver from under his coat. "You do a good job now, hear?" he said. "Or we'll shoot you."

It took all my aplomb to say, "Hey, put that away! Don't make the tattoo artist nervous."

"Naw, Gus," said Alex, and put his hand on his brother's arm. "Put it away."

Gus finally did. Alex turned to me and grinned. "Don't mind him," he said. "Gus is trigger-happy when he's drunk. Shoots anything in sight."

This was scarcely a remark calculated to make the tattoo artist less nervous. For the next thirty minutes, while they made on the chair the hundred little movements that the drunk always does, I had to tattoo these examples of Chicago's finest. The worst thing was that Gus kept drawing his gun from time to time and pointing it at my stomach while I was trying to tattoo him, and doing the same thing while I was working on his brother. I kept pushing the barrel aside, somehow maintaining an outward calm and telling him not to move, not to make me nervous, and giving him other sensible, heartfelt injunctions, in which his brother joined. They had little effect on Gus. At long last the tattoos were finished. I collected my four dollars, and they left.

I closed the curtains and sank into the chair, trembling. The delayed reaction made me actually unable to move for several minutes. Frank, the handsome Lithuanian arcade manager, hearing no voices nor needles buzzing, came to see what was wrong. I told him.

"The bastards," he said, over and over. "The dirty bastards. Why dint you call me?"

I moistened dry lips. "They'd probably have shot you for sure,"

I said. "Just what the hell can a person do with a drunk cop waving a gun?"

Frank paused. "Not a heluva lot," he said.

I had a few nightmares for several weeks.

There was one alcoholic cop named John on the south State Street beat. He had a sweet collection racket going and every month would come around for his payoff. I was not doing anything wrong; it was just John's way of supplementing his income. He never smelled sober, and his violet-colored Irish nose was a tangled web of broken veins and pustules. His whole face was plum-colored. If I did not pay (this before I learned what he wanted) he would merely come into the shop and stand there flat-footedly. His presence kept the shop empty. Most of the city-boys had guilty consciences; they would see him and stay away while he was there. I refused at first to pay his petty "protection" fee of ten bucks until he asked me directly. And then I paid—and for ten years thereafter. Everyone on the street hated him, but everyone paid. He was finally hospitalized and removed from the force.

Other cops who got tattooed (John had none) were mostly young, and most of them honest; some of them had already been tattooed while in a military service. One was Jim, a patrolman from the South side of Chicago. He was friendly to talk with, and had about a dozen tattoos. He was unhappily married, however, or his wife was frigid. He was fond of dressing in civvies—but always with his gun—and coming to south State Street to see what girls he could pick up. If he couldn't find a woman he would avail himself of one of the many homosexuals who cruised south State.

There was another Jim, not so well-adjusted. This one had been fired from the Milwaukee force, had two tattoos, was the father of a boy, was divorced, and generally lived beyond his means. This second Jim was troubled with impotence with both women and men, but seemed to have a special appeal for homosexuals. He came in one night proudly displaying a hundred-dollar bill which he had "earned" for an hour with a gay guy. He spent five of his hundred on the design of a little skunk holding a flower, the one that we call "Lil Stinker," under which he wanted written "My son, Jim," the name of his child.

Two other cops puzzled me with their requests for tattoos of scars. One wanted a five-inch scar complete with red cross-stitch lines; the other wanted one tattooed around his left nipple in a horseshoe shape. I did not know for what purpose the scars were intended, but told both of them that such a "scar" would certainly never fool a doctor. Perhaps they wanted them merely to buttress one of their tall tales.

All in all I did not have much trouble with the police, either local or federal. One FBI field man named Bill visited me with the photo of an AWOL soldier who was heavily tattooed.

"Ever seen him before?" Bill asked.

"No," I said, looking at the tattoos. "But if you'll go up and ask Art in the Super-Arcade he might be able to help you. He put on this one and this one."

Bill was astounded. "You mean to say that you can identify each other's work?"

"Yes," I said, "if we're in the same part of the country and see enough of the kind of work the other fellow does."

Bill could hardly believe it. It set up a fascination in him for tattooing and he spent many hours in the shop talking. He even suggested that I give a short talk to the FBI field men detailing this means of identification, but then he got shot and killed and nothing came of his proposal.

LOVELY LADIES, TRAMPS, DYKES, AND FARM WIVES

When I finally discovered the trouble that always surrounded the tattooing of women, I established a policy of refusing to tattoo a woman unless she were twenty-one, married and accompanied by her husband, with documentary proof to show their marriage. The only exception to this was the lesbians, and they had to be over twenty-one and prove it. In those tight and unpermissive 1950s, too many scenes with irate husbands, furious parents, indignant boyfriends, and savage lovers made it necessary to accept female customers only with great care.

It has already been noted that one of the most frequent questions asked by the young men who came into the shop was "Do women ever come in here for tattoos?" to which my answer was "Yes, occasionally."

"Where do they get 'em?" was next.

"Right where you're thinking," was the answer, and then perhaps would follow the story of the whore and the swallow-tail butterfly at her celestial gate. Then I might add: "But nice girls don't get tattooed," to which they agreed in a half-disappointed way. But to amuse the sailors who asked about women I sometimes responded with a titillating old word-play: "Actually, I don't like to tattoo women. I usually go in the hole on those jobs."

In the years of tattooing in Chicago I put a tattoo on only one really beautiful girl. The rest were large lank-haired skags, with ruined landscapes of faces and sagging hose and run-over heels.

The one beautiful girl was a strip-teaser from the old Showboat Lounge nearby. She came in — very vital and pretty and young — accompanied by a nebbish male and a skinny broken-down bag of a B-girl.

"I've always wanted a tattoo," she said. "Put one on."

Everyone tried to dissuade her, the nebbish young man making negative signs at me behind her back. I tried to talk her out of it, but no go.

Finally I said, "How high are you at the moment?"

"Honey," she said with a dazzling smile, "I been high all my life." Wherewith she chased the others away to the far side of the screen, whooped up her dress, pulled down her black lace panties and bent slightly forward with her hands on her upper thighs, her legs apart. She reached back and slapped herself on the butt. "There!" she said. "Put the name 'Slats'!"

So I did, feeling somewhat distracted by everything, but managing to control myself long enough to print the word nicely, remembering the old dirty joke about pulling out hairs and being a gentleman.

The lesbians were another matter. Whenever they came in they frightened the sailors and many of the city-boys out of the shop. I did not relish their arrival nor particularly want their business. The "butch" one was usually fat as a pig, in slacks, which from behind made her butt look like two little boys fighting under a blanket. The "male" ones had mannish haircuts and bellowed. In a sense they were no different from the boys getting their girl-friends' names on them. That was all they wanted, perhaps with a little floral design, and then they wanted their name on the "lady" of the pair.

One odd and exhausting couple was from Milwaukee. The butch one wanted a skull with a motorcycle cap on the inside of her right forearm; she had about twenty tattoos scattered over herself in various places. Her smell was stomach-churning; I doubted that she had bathed in months. Above the skull she wanted "Parker's Raiders" printed, the name of a motorcycle gang, of which I presumed she belonged to the ladies' auxiliary. Then she wanted a dagger above her knee re-done, and had "Death Before Dishonor" printed around that. In later life in California I would become accustomed to working on the "old ladies" of Hells Angels, but this woman—I believe—came to me even before the Hells Angels existed.

She returned a few days later to show them to me and ask why the surrounding flesh had turned black and blue. I explained that feminine flesh was so delicate and bruised so easily that such discoloration was to be always expected with tattoos on women. She still hadn't bathed. Even though I saturated the air after she left with the Fuller Brush "Hollyberry" spray, the stench of rotting aqueducts remained for hours.

In the early days I did not watch TV, but there was one movie or show that had as a "piquant detail" of the plot the tattooing of a small butterfly on a woman's shoulder. The effect that show had on a number of farm wives in Illinois was amazing. At least fifteen drifted in within two months after the TV showing, and each wanted a small butterfly on the right shoulder blade. Lacking in sophistication and hardly understanding their motives, these women were invariabily accompanied by their farmer husbands who stood by—generally approving—while the wife got her butterfly. It was a momentary fad equaled only by the demand among young men for a rose tattoo on the chest, following the movie of *The Rose Tattoo* by Tennessee Williams.

The farm women were to be somewhat pitied, and in imagination

I could hear the gossip of their neighbors' wives: "Imagine . . . that damfool Sally . . . a-gittin' a *tat*too jes' like a big-city whore!"

One of those women came in with her husband and a daughter, aged twelve. When daughter saw what mama got, she wanted one too — a rose high on her thigh. I tried to convince her parents it was not a thing for a young girl to get, but since parental consent — even encouragement — was there, she got it. That would have been the right moment for a Chicago cop to have walked in. I doubt that parental consent would have saved me.

The appearance of any woman in the shop was always a matter of concern for me. If there were boys present they often forgot that women were there too, and their language usually contained obscenities. One woman who was peering around the shop once complained loudly about the coarse sailor-talk. (This was, after all, the 1950s, and the Modern Woman had not yet undergone her change into Virginia Slim.)

"If you were gentlemen," she said belligerently to a crowd of eight or nine sailors, "you wouldn't talk that way in front of a lady."

I saw the embarrassment of the young sailors, so I said in my hardest neo-academic tone, "Madame, if you were a lady you wouldn't be in a tattoo shop."

The boys' laughter drove her out, red-faced with fury.

ODDS AND ENDS

There were many characters who did not fit into any of the preceding categories — some of them extremely interesting or boring or unusual in one another.

One of the oddest was a person from Milwaukee whom I privately called the "Ancient Motorcyclist." At an age — mid-fifties — when most good men are settled and have put away childish things, this cat was still hanging each lumpish half of his great gluteus maximus over the sides of his bike-seat, and wearing regalia of full leather . . . very strange in 1954.

He was repulsive to begin with. His almost hairless puffy face-skin was a kind of pale yellow hue, plump, and covered with a network of tiny interlocking wrinkles. A medico could have diagnosed his ailment immediately as Froelich's syndrome, with the pale blue eyes, the almost albino coloring and pale yellow hair, the tendency to adipose hairless skin, and possibly cryptorchidism, though I never discovered that.

He hove into the shop one night when I was still in the old arcade. Somehow his appearance awakened in me the "Doctor Fell" reaction, as a student memorialized his professor at the University of Edinburgh long ago: "I do not like thee, Doctor Fell /And why it is I cannot tell;/ I only know so very well / I do not like thee, Doctor Fell."

His complete leather costume included a motorcycle cap with yellow wing symbol, the cap held on with a gaucho cord beneath his chin. He also carried a yellow crash helmet with a yellow chin strap. He wore green-tinted glasses of the wrap-around kind, a much-decorated leather jacket with a profusion of metallic and jeweled studs sprinkled over it, a heavy wide "kidney" belt with three buckles, blue jeans bursting over fat thighs, and boots decorated almost as much as his jacket, with chains across the instep and studs on the heels. A younger man might have got away with wearing such a costume. This was in the mid 1950s and the world was not yet used to the s/m syndrome [by which one might mean either "Sado-Masochistic" or "Standing and Modeling"] nor to motorcycle cultists.

It did not take him long to reveal that he was homosexual; the thousand little signs were obvious enough. And when the handsome young Earl of the "Road Wolves" came in together with one of his "sickle" buddies, both of them wearing leather jackets, the glittering eye and the lust-look appeared in the seamed and wrinkled face of the Ancient Motorcyclist. For a while there was a good deal of technical talk about bikes, and then the Ancient Motorcyclist tried to break up the two, who were not riding that evening, by offering Earl a lift north on his motorcycle.

During a moment when the Ancient One walked away, I said "Better watch out for him."

"You t'ink we're stupid?" Earl said. "We know what he is."

"I don't want this shop used to make dates with young men," I said, secretly tickled as I wondered what Earl might do if I added "by anyone except myself."

"Don't worry about a t'ing," said Earl.

They amused themselves by leading the motorcyclist on, and then finally left by themselves. The Ancient One's frustration was complete. He had been hanging around for about three hours and his sly insinuations were superficial and tiresome.

It grew late, and time to close the shop. He had been hinting about having something on his dingdong in a green outline — a green snake. At that early stage I had not had much experience tattooing dingdongs. But I had at least discovered that the organ had a life of its own, and frequently surprised its owner. When the needle approached, it would squirm and try to recede into the belly, turning to soft rubber. You had to put a second finger underneath on the urethra and push upwards, while with the index finger and thumb you pulled down on each side to tighten the skin so that it would receive the needle. To put a snake around the organ was mechanically so difficult that I was dismayed at the prospect.

I was saved, however, from this impossible task.

"And while you're doing it," the Ancient Motorcyclist said, "I want you to handcuff me to the bench so I can't move."

My temper flared, and I took on the outraged moralizing attitude of a hypocritical televangelist. "What the goddamned hell do you think I'm here for?" I said violently. "There's no time for fun and games in this shop. A green snake around it would just be a ragged green line. Besides, you can't outline in green, only in black. Go somewhere else for your silly pastimes."

At that moment Frank, the handsome Lithuanian manager of the arcade, appeared, having heard my loud talk.

"What's goin' on here?" he said. Then he addressed the Ancient One. "What do you want?"

I told him.

Frank scowled at the man. "You been hangin' around here for hours," he said. "Why you come up with a thing like that right at closin' time?"

The motorcyclist muttered something.

"I guess you'd better get out of here," I said. "You've told me several times you thought the Preacher did better work, and he may not be busy now."

The Ancient Motorcyclist left in a great huff, and burdened us no more.

* * * *

Another one was Bill, the tattooed harpist. Late one winter evening he came into the shop, a tall lean handsome guy dressed in full leather. He eyed me and then sort of crept crablike and sidewise around the room.

"I-I think I'd l-l-like a t-t-t-tattoo," he said. He stammered so badly that it was difficult to understand him, and very painful to listen to; I kept trying deep in my own vocal cords to help him get his voice going. At times he had to abandon one word entirely and choose a synonym.

He chose a large black panther, crawling up his right biceps to his shoulder. Over a few months I put five big pieces on him — a large ferocious green dragon on his left biceps, a snake fighting an eagle on one forearm, and on the other a specially designed dagger with eagle, an American shield, and "Death Before Dishonor" to top it off. A final chest-piece was a widespread eagle.

Bill was extremely interesting. A month away from getting a Master's degree at the University of Michigan — in Latin and Greek, of all things — he had suddenly departed and come to Chicago where he got a job delivering something or other on a three-wheeled motorcycle. He had mother-trouble, and was completely dominated by her. Like many uncomprehending females she laughed at him, shamed him in front of others, and called him a failure. No wonder he stammered.

Bill bought a motorcycle as a rebellion-symbol, since she hated them; and then further to jolt his companions, he bought a harp on installments — a great huge concert harp, a monster all full of goldleaf and baroque scrollwork and bunches of grapes — the whole shebang. He told me that the shock value of it when he brought a trick home was worth twice the price he was paying for it.

I lent him a copy of *Gracian's Manual*, and one evening we went for pizza and cola and then to his house where we talked for three hours about his problems, his mother, his sex-life, and all the rest.

It was surprising to get a phone call from him the next morning. All the stammering was gone! He told me of his resolve to sell his furniture, and move with his harp to New York City. The motorcycle had already disappeared because of a serious accident he had. I was uneasy about the permanence of his "cure"; those sudden transformations often slipped. But he went to New York, completely cutting the silver cord. How much therapeutic value the tattoos had for helping him to readjust is a matter best left to the psychiatrists, but I believe it was considerable.

*   *   *   *   *

Then there was Pete, a light-skinned black, a very intelligent but alcoholic cat. Pete was a brain. He worked for the government and was taking additional courses so that he could become a teacher in the Chicago public schools. This was all the more astonishing since he had a record as an ex-convict; he had been able to hide the fact successfully from the school authorities. He wrote beatnik and far-out poetry, and I mortally wounded him by not taking his poetic efforts very seriously. Pete was in love with tattooing, especially when he was drinking, and I put four or five large designs on him.

Pete told perhaps the wildest stories of any of my customers, and I sadly suspect that most of them were true. He had been in jail in Ohio, and had once had a fight with the jail's leader-convict, a tough cookie who turned all the other cons against Pete. There was only one solution that Pete could see. During a movie one night he crawled on the floor between the rows of prisoners, carrying a brick in a sock, and when he reached the boss, rose up behind him and bashed in his head. "Like a mushmelon," he laughed. "It was either him or me."

"What happened afterwards?" I asked.

"Nothing. Everybody hated him. He had no family. They shipped his body back to New Jersey and things were pretty peaceful after that."

"What will they ever do to you if they find out a teacher is an ex-con?"

He shrugged. "How can they? I wasn't fingerprinted for the teaching job."

Pete became increasingly violent towards me, largely because he could make no visible impression on me, and because I would not take his intellect seriously enough. On several occasions when he came into the shop drunk, belligerent, and physically violent, I actually feared for my life. I even gave word to some friends that if anything happened to me, they might consider its cause to be Pete.

*   *   *   *   *

The advertisement that I carried in the yellow pages of the telephone book added to my "respectability" and set me apart from the transient jaggers who worked in the arcades up the street. But I suppose that the ad probably brought me no more than twelve customers in all the years I maintained it. Tattooing seemed to be exclusively a "drop-in" business, or else my clients could not read or were too stupid to think of the yellow pages.

Many of the telephone calls were from persons asking about removals, and they were given one standard answer: go to a doctor. But there were many crank calls. During one pre-holiday season while I was still in the old arcade, a man called to say that he wanted to give his friend an unusual Christmas present, and did I issue gift certificates for a tattoo? I said that it could be arranged. Then he went on to ask if it were possible to have it anywhere on the body, and he gradually worked around to the genitals. At that point I began to notice an odd kind of breathlessness in his voice, and a kind of rhythmic jerkiness to his speech. My naiveté vanished in a puff, and I knew that he was sitting at home jacking off.

It was the first of many such calls, and afterwards all questions about genital tattooing were stopped with: "I'm sorry—I don't discuss such details over the phone. You'll have to come into the shop." But not many came . . .

There were other calls—some from irate mothers accusing me of tattooing their underage children; these I turned aside by giving them the phone numbers of other arcades up the street, and righteously disclaiming any guilt, explaining—if they gave me time— my system of making sure the customer was eighteen.

One summer afternoon the phone rang and a voice said, "This is Marlin Perkins." The name was well-known: Perkins was curator of the Lincoln Park Zoo, and a TV personality.

"How do you do," I said. "I am Percy B. Shelley."

He laughed. "No, it really is Marlin Perkins," he said. "We have a little problem here at the zoo."

I apologized and said that there were many crank calls. He went on to explain that they had been giving medication to a number of their snakes that had fallen ill, and wanted to identify which ones had been given certain medications, and could they be tattooed with some kind of small identifying symbol?

"I-I d-don't know," I stuttered. "I've never done such work before."

"Would you be willing to try?" he asked. "In some spots the scales are rather soft, and under the mouth might be a good place. And then we could do the rest of the work if you will tell us where to buy the proper equipment."

"I'll t-try," I said. "I hope however that you'll hold the beast."

The next afternoon he appeared, holding a pillowcase with something weighty at the bottom of it—something that moved a little while I watched. I had meanwhile dug out my oldest strongest needle, the one I used to put owner's marks on pedigreed dogs occasionally, and sat sweating and ready.

He was very nice and reassuring about it. It was a small deadly coral snake. My hand shook as much as it did when I put on my first tattoo. I remember the open mouth, the flickering tongue, and a hand holding the head steady and upside down. I plunged the needle in, and it penetrated without great difficulty.

I don't remember if I charged him anything for it. I do recall that I went into the back room, took a tranquilizer, and lay down to rest for an hour.

Tattooing furnished me with a kind of continuing drama, exciting, odd, and unusual, and quickly spoiled me for any kind of dull workaday routine occupation. It was that—and the money—that addicted me to the business. After a few years of such experiences, it would not have been possible ever to sit at a desk again from nine to five, or to teach, or to hold down any job demanding either physical or mental labor of an ordinary kind. The unusual clientele— always different, always changing—kept me fascinated and swimming in the mainstream of life—certainly in its dark rich depths. At times there was boredom, of course, and repeatedly answering the same questions was tiresome. But each person was a new and challenging problem, a human being moved by desires and longings and frustrations which he could often not comprehend, or only dimly perceive. For anyone with even the mildest interest in people, tattooing was an ideal occupation. And you never had to go cruising the bars and the baths, looking for beauty . . .

. . . it came to you.

PART VII

Barnacles and Leeches

In all the locations where I have tattooed, there has always been a certain type of individual haunting the shop. Sometimes they have already been tattooed, but most of them have not. These are the "hangers-on," persons usually without visible means of support, or perhaps with minor jobs. A tattoo shop seems to exert a peculiar type of fascination for them. Some wanted to learn how to tattoo, others just wanted to listen and talk. Most were not very bright; their brains could be exhaustively probed in a half-hour's conversation, and after that everything was simply repetition. Their vocabularies seemed to contain about a hundred words, most of them obscene.

Among the hangers-on and part-time workers at the old arcade there was Bob—a balding red-haired hillbilly with a vulgar mind and a foul tongue, full of little mountain rimes and "smart sayings" that he thought cute, and used over and over. He had the morals of a muskrat and a con man's complete lack of ethics, always out for a fast and easy buck. I never opened the shop until noon, and Bob would send the potential morning customers across the street to Shaky Jake, because Jake gave him a dollar for each one referred. I tried to get him to tell them to come back at noon, but he would only grin and say: "Well, a guy's gotta make a buck, ain't he?"

One episode tells much about him. A soldier getting a tattoo from me suddenly got woozy and had to go back to the john to throw up. Shaken, white, and sweating, he returned to be bandaged, and then left. Within a half-hour he was back, saying that he had left his wallet on the washbowl. Bob was the only one in the arcade that evening. With a certain sad realization I went with the soldier back to the washroom. No sign of the wallet.

"Where is it?" I asked Bob. "Did you see it?"

He shrugged. "There's been a half-dozen people in here in the last half-hour," he said.

A lie. Anyone coming in had to pass my shack. There had been no one.

All I could do was take the soldier's name and tell him that if it were found, I'd send it to him. The kid was shaken, because he had two weeks' pay in it, about thirty dollars. As soon as he left I accused Bob.

"What the hell," he said. "The kid doesn't need the money as much as I do."

Bob was the Compleat Ladies' Man and had an almost continuous case of gonorrhea, which he referred to as another "rose tattoo." He already had a few clumsily executed markings here and there, self-applied while in the pokey. He was afraid to have any more, but he finally succumbed to the design of a large green dragon that I had put on several persons.

"Chee," he said, "gimme one like dat, will yuh, Phil?"

"After all you've done for me?" I said. "Like sending customers to Jake?"

"Aw hell," he said, "don't be that way. Think of the times I've swept out your joint. Besides," he said, "I'll give you five dollars." The price was thirty.

"Okay," I said, a plan forming. "Where you want it?"

He gave me the five. "On my chest," he said.

As a novice I had not yet learned that chest work should be done with the customer lying down. It was easier that way for both him and the tattooist. Fainting was not nearly so likely, and the ink in the needles flowed downward better. But I did not yet have a slanted bench. Bob sat in a chair.

"Never irritate a tattoo artist *before* he tattoos you" is an old adage that all should know. And laymen are unaware that the artist can manage any one of several different "touches" ranging from light to heavy, or that he can adjust the needle-length from short to long, or rev up the machines to move faster.

Thinking of the soldier and his thirty dollars, I adjusted my needles . . . and then began.

Poor Bob! What a racket he made! How he huffed and puffed,

and how the sweat rolled off him to puddle on the blue oilcloth cushion! Then he fainted. I poured some water on his head and brought him back.

"Just relax," I said, holding him upright. He was chalk-white and trembling.

"Not now," he managed to gasp. " . . . finish it later."

"I haven't even got the outline done."

". . . can't," he muttered and reeled off towards the back of the arcade to lie down and recover.

I felt the soldier had been repaid in some sort of coin, even though he would never be able to spend it.

Bob's tattoo was never finished. Perhaps to this day it remains in outline form on his pimpled chest with its sparse red hair. After he was fired from his part-time job in the arcade for rifling the machines, he came back only once about five years later, this time to my new shop across the street, and asked to borrow two bucks. I told him I didn't have it. He hung around for quite a while and then said, "Tell you what: I'll give you a blowjob for two bucks."

"Not interested," I said. "And what's happened to you? When did you change? I thought you were nuts about women."

He shrugged. "Guess I always been queer," he said.

"Used the cunt business to hide it, I suppose—or didn't you know?"

"Guess I dint know," he said. "Gimme a coupla cigarettes anyway."

I gave him what was left in a package and never saw him after that.

*   *   *   *   *

Then there was Tommy. Poor Tommy was not quite right in the head. He came into the shop first with a few of the "Road Wolves," although he was not a member.

"Too stupid," one of them said in front of him, and another added: "He's really crazy."

And with that, right in the shop, Tommy, aged seventeen, stood up to his height of six-feet-three, took the offender by the throat, and started to choke him until we pulled him off.

"Don't nobody never call me crazy and get away with it!" he yelled.

We quieted him eventually, largely with the promise of another tattoo. He already had four or five, most of them put on by Randy — hideous work with lots of lumpish scar tissue from deep digging.

Tommy finally became one of "my boys," transferring his allegiance from Randy. After I put my first one on his dingdong, on his eighteenth birthday, he never got one from anyone else, proud of being "faithful" to me.

He was a tall handsome Pole from a broken family, and he gradually told me the story of his life — with great reluctance. In the shop there were many examples of what someone once called "the terrible blinding beauty of the uneducated." Tommy had it.

But that was all he had. More than anything else he wanted to join the Marines. He had been rejected because of two flaws: he had little intelligence, and he had a slightly pointed sternum of the kind called "pigeon-breasted."

Tommy resented the use of the word "crazy," hated it with a frenzy. As a child he had had what he called a nervous breakdown; he had been subjected either to insulin shock or electrotherapy — he didn't know which. He had been fired from numerous jobs because he literally did not know the difference between addition and subtraction, nor what an inch was, nor how many in a foot. Time after time, as he went on one of his visits to take the military intelligence exams, I worked with him until I finally gave up. In the three pounds of dimly conscious meat which was his brain there were only four drives: food, liquor, money, and sex. Later on he satisfied all of them by becoming a male hustler, but he could not even do that well, because he often jackrolled his tricks and the word got around.

For six years he went steadily downhill, gradually losing his good looks as he moved into his twenties. The final time he returned he had become a falwell and had really gone over the edge; his loose rambling talk about heaven and hell and God never stopped. He ended in a state mental hospital from which he wrote to me asking me to become his sponsor so that he could get out. But had I taken care of all the lame dogs who came to me for help during the tattoo years, it would have been myself in the asylum, not they.

* * * * *

Another hanger-on inherited from Randy was Jack, a slight nervous boy of nineteen with already thinning black hair. Out of his basic insecurity he had already been much tattooed with Randy's deeply scarring inept work.

More than any other hanger-on Jack terrified me at first, before he transferred his fidelity from Randy, who hated me with a passion. And Randy and Jack were as thick as the thieves they actually were. To me Jack seemed to be a kind of dangerous extension of Randy. He was not a typical juvenile delinquent; he came from a very wealthy family in Oak Park, his father being the owner of a large roofing company. Later, when Jack went bonkers from the goofballs and bennies and stuff he was shooting up the mainline, the father came to ask me how long I had known of Jack's habit. The old man buried his face in his hands, weeping, and muttered "What did I do wrong?"

I tried to tell him it was not his fault, but I feared it was . . .

Randy had been teaching Jack how to tattoo, and Jack had put many crude black-only designs on his own legs, where he could reach to stretch the skin and do them. He finally talked Randy into putting on his back a large panther and snake struggling, but the pain was such that Randy had to stop, leaving a poorly done thing full of scar tissue. After Jack had "transferred" to me, we tried to change the design into the large head of a Japanese geisha, but once again the pain forced Jack to call a halt.

Jack wanted desperately to be bad. He studied the attitudes of his buddies, delinquents and ex-cons alike, and copied their gestures. But the movements never came off exactly right. When he got started on marijuana he was always bringing me a "nickel's worth" but it was poor stuff and did nothing except make me sleepy. I gave it away to others.

Like so many of his friends, Jack thrived on violence. One of his buddies was Ted, who earlier had been sent away for three years for a holdup involving violence, and for making a snarling threat at the judge who sentenced him. One evening Jack brought in a bloody handkerchief with something wrapped in it. His sly little weasel face was grinning widely. "You want somebody beat up?" he asked. "I was out with Ted and that's the way he gets his kicks."

He unrolled the sopping handkerchief and showed me eight broken teeth, and said proudly, enviously, "Ted knocked 'em out of a guy he robbed. He'll take care of anybody you want for fifty bucks."

The sight unnerved me so much that the room began to swim, and I put my head down so that I wouldn't faint, pretending to tie my shoe lace.

"N-no thanks," I finally said. "I can't afford it."

Jack grinned and wrapped up the teeth again and stuck the bloody trophy in his pocket.

What does one do in such a case? Inform the police? Tattoo artists had of necessity to keep the secrets of the confessional, as did priests, psychiatrists, and doctors—but not for their ethical reasons; ours were kept more out of an instinct of self-preservation. My conscience troubled me severely on several occasions. Should I have told Jack's father about his downhill progress? When the old man finally confronted me and I had to admit I had known about it, I had a hard time justifying my silence.

After marijuana—or rather during, because he never stopped smoking from ten to twelve joints a day—he went on to bennies, and thence to barbiturates. His consumption was terrific; he really preferred amphetamines, taking as many as forty or fifty ten milligram tablets a day. In the shop he was sometimes so high he fell over chairs and stools, and even lay flat on the floor. He could no longer hold a water glass or pencil because his hands shook so violently. Even after his hospitalization for amphetamine addiction (he never reached the "hard" stage of heroin), he was back on them two weeks after his release. He got them from unscrupulous druggists in the Chicago area who sold him the pills in lots of a thousand.

Jack got married and had two children. His wife Lorrie was as punchy as he was, and she once came to my house to borrow ten dollars. When Jack later repaid me, he told me that I was lucky—that Lorrie had come to case the joint, so that her current boy friend could come back later and rob me.

*   *   *   *   *

One of the most persistent and eventually annoying hangers-on was an older fellow named Fred, who also fancied himself a tattoo artist and dreamed of the day he would "begin." Fred was of German stock, had a big frame, and was almost completely covered with tattoos, save for his calves on which during World War II he had developed some sort of skin parasite that he called "jungle rot." The Preacher had done most of his work.

Fred liked to build and make things. He had a full set of tattoo instruments, and was continually borrowing my stencils and designs to copy them. Unfortunately the man had no artistic talent and could no more draw than be faithful to his wife. He was one of those in whom a developed allegiance lasts a long time; it was well over three years before I could get rid of him entirely. This, however, could be tolerated, because when it came time to leave the old Sportland Arcade and move across the street to the new quarters, it was Fred who helped me build the shop—putting up partitions, sawing this and that, building a workbench and cabinet with twenty stencil drawers, and doing all the heavy work that lay beyond my own interests, inclinations, and abilities. He even constructed a power-pack that worked better than any power-source I had ever used.

In return for his services, he asked only that he be tattooed occasionally. He wanted his small bare spots filled in, or the background color between his innumerable designs changed. He was about fifty years old, very gentle and soft-spoken, save when someone commented in some way on his age or appearance; he looked much older than he was. He worked in a freight-handling office for one of the railroads, and during the day had a part-time job at Marshall Field's. Thus he had an interval of three hours every afternoon, and they were spent, alas, at my shop.

Fred had a grossly fat wife, and a son and daughter; they were Catholic but he was not. He was a Mason and later became a Shriner, but the hard study the latter required was very painful for him, since he had no academic training of any kind. I learned to look on him as a fixture, in the same way you notice an article of furniture—and then walk around it—because an hour with him was enough to exhaust his not very profound personality.

After three years of this "devotion" to my shop and myself, he suddenly came no more, transferring his allegiance to another tattooist, Ralph, up the street. But Ralph died and Fred was left without any spot to spend his three empty afternoon hours. He had left a good deal of his stuff in my shop, and he re-appeared once to pick it up and make a kind of clumsy effort to re-transfer his fealty. But something was wrong with me that day—probably the lunch I had eaten—and I was frosty with him. After that one half-hearted attempt he disappeared completely. He had been a good friend of Dietzel, the old grand master tattooist in Milwaukee because they were both Shriners, but the Old Master forsook him also when he learned that Fred—under wife-pressure and the fact that his son was studying to be a priest—had been toying with the idea of becoming a Catholic.

Fred could give no reason why he was covered with tattoos beyond "Oh, I think they're purty." From what he told me over the years, the young svelte girl he had married was perhaps partly responsible for it; as she grew fat and developed diabetes and would never allow Fred to touch her, who can say to what pleasures he turned? Perhaps to the lonely and morose delight of viewing his colorful and sumptuous self as he lolled in the hot water of his tub, locked securely away from her, enchanted by the sight of the bright macaws and green dragons and clowns, all sparkling like jewels under the brightening effect of the hot water? What were his dreams and fantasies? Looking at himself may have helped lighten the burden of his life.

*   *   *   *   *

Even more persistent than Fred was an ex-con named Roy Robinson. Beyond doubt Roy was the most morally and ethically rotten person I had ever known. He had a classic case of anomia—no morals at all—and would have been easily recognized by any psychiatrist as a true sociopath. He never developed any loyalties to anyone no matter what was done for him, and he never learned anything from punishment. His difficulty may have stemmed largely from a loveless childhood and a low-class broken home. He was a good example of the truth in the old wives' saying that "if you do not stroke a child enough his backbone will shrivel."

Roy was about twenty-seven, six-feet-two, and toothless. Three sets of dentures had either been broken in his escapades, or lost, and finally he gave up bothering with teeth. He had been arrested nearly eighty times and spent a good third of his life in prison. He had a kind of Walter Mitty mind, though slightly more realistic than poor befuddled Tommy's; he was always *waiting* for something good to happen to him. It never did. Instead, to hear him tell it, he was bad-luck-prone. Someone was always beating him or robbing him, or he was always getting caught; he fell down stairs and got black eyes and other wounds and cuts regularly. He had a passion for watches of all kinds, and rings and cigarette lighters. Everything I gave him soon disappeared. It took me at least five of the seven years I knew him to discover that he had not lost them, as he claimed, but had pawned them.

He was tattooed on both arms, and had a small one over his heart. Much of the work he had on him had been begun in the pokey, and finished by professionals during his time on the outside. He was a great liar; you could never believe a word he said, but it took me a long time to discover that, too. He had been married two or three times, his last one a very ugly woman who made his life hectic. He was a strange kind of alcoholic: one bottle of beer made him obnoxiously talkative, and removed what small control he had over himself. He was very fond of "the gurls," but that did not keep him from having a regular clientele of homosexuals whom he actively serviced for amounts ranging from two to ten dollars; he took the money thus earned and spent it on his women. He had a remarkable tongue; with his teeth not in the way he could extend it to touch the tip of his nose or chin, and then flick it sideways. He said that his gurls—and boys—loved it.

His hardluck stories were remarkable, and he was always penniless. He insinuated himself into my shop-existence by sweeping out the place, scrubbing and mopping the floors, helping me with odd jobs, and running errands. Gradually I came to depend on "ole Roy" and even grew to be warily fond of him. But in all the years of knowing him, I never could trust him to be alone in the front of the shop while I was in the back, or vice versa. He stole from me just as easily and with no more compunction than he jackrolled a stranger.

The only serious burglary in the shop was committed by him. When I opened my place one Saturday morning, I discovered a drawer from the filing cabinet in the middle of the floor, the locks broken off all the hasps, and a general disarray. The burglars had been fairly considerate. They took a cupful of quarters—about $25 worth—which I used to make change for the customers, and also swiped a pair of binoculars. It was amazing that they did not take the typewriter and radio. But investigation showed that they had entered from the shack behind the shop, sliding down a walled-up window-well from the floor above. On the climb back a burglar could not be burdened with bulky objects.

The blame fell naturally on Roy whom I did not see again for two years. One of his sexual clients called me a month after the burglary to ask where he was; he told me that Roy had tried to sell him a pair of binoculars some time ago, just before he left for Florida—where, it turned out, he would spend two years in Raiford prison.

With the bravado and brass of the born-bad ones, Roy showed up again after his release, and denied everything. It was perhaps not so much the fascination of tattooing that made him a hanger-on as the sweet smell of money. Like a water-witch he could sense its presence, no matter how little or deeply buried. But he ended up—in search, perhaps, of another more final kind of security—jumping into Lake Michigan and drowning himself.

These few persons were typical of the scores of habitués that frequented the shop during the Chicago years. Their motivations were sometimes transparent, sometimes obscure. Every tattoo artist has had the same experience. What these people were looking for, what they wanted and how they reacted, all contributed to the mystery and the fascination of the life.

PART VIII

Excuses —
Mine and Theirs, Before and After

The commonest excuse to be heard for a tattoo is usually "I got drunk and the next morning I woke up and had this tattoo." It is usually given as a kind of shamefaced explanation for the tattoo, especially if it is poorly executed.

Such an evasion is hardly ever true. There are of course many tattoo artists who will work on someone no matter how drunk that person is, but those with some ethics or pride in workmanship never would. There are many reasons for refusing to work on someone who has had too much to drink.

In the first place, a drunk cannot sit still. If you tell him this, he protests loudly that he can. But he cannot. A drunk is in continual motion—either weaving back and forth on the chair or making unpredictable movements with his hands, feet, or body, such as turning to ask someone for a cigarette. His arms are never still. You might have a good solid grip on the biceps on which he is getting the tattoo, but suddenly he will move the other arm, and you may make a mistake. Such errors are hard to erase or conceal.

Again, if it happens to be the customer's first tattoo, he is already subconsciously frightened. If he has also been drinking he is very likely to get sick suddenly and vomit in your lap or on the floor. This had to happen only once to me, for "No tattoos on persons who have had too much to drink" to become an iron rule. The sign on the wall was simply pointed to when a drunk requested a tattoo. It had one more line: "I am the only judge of your condition." But I never objected to someone having a drink or two to bolster his courage.

Another reason for refusing drunks was that their judgment was often so clouded by booze that the choice of design selected was regretted as soon as they became sober. Perhaps, also, the tattoo artist might get into trouble. One of the syndicate jaggers once put a tattoo on a woman who came in with an army sergeant. The next day a stranger showed up with the same woman, who now had a black eye. "Did you put this tattoo on my wife last night?" the man bellowed.

The jagger looked at it and was forced to admit he had. "You got somebody else's name in it!" the husband shouted.

And then the tattoo artist had a black eye, too.

My shop was always closed early because I wanted to avoid the drunks, who usually arrived much later than the others. They would begin to drift in about eleven; I always tried to be gone by ten. Sometimes I had to stay longer if customers were waiting, and there was often trouble with the snockered ones.

But only about one in twenty was too drunk to be worked on. Thus the excuse that "I got drunk and woke up with one" was perhaps manufactured out of a mild sense of shame or embarrassment or guilt for having a tattoo at all. Tattooing, because of the tension and the pain involved—negligible for some persons with a high threshold, and intense for others—was really a great aid in sobering a person. An ex-Navy chief once told me that while he was in the service it was a common thing for a crowd of mildly drunken sailors to say to each other, "Let's go get a tattoo and sober up."

Several reasons for not getting tattoos have already been considered: pain fears, desire to keep the body unmarked, social stigma, and so on. But occasionally there were other excuses.

Often I heard a sailor say: "Not me—I ain't gonna get a tattoo. If God had intended me to have one, I'd've been born with one."

This usually brought out a waspish "If that's true, why do you cut your fingernails or get a haircut? If you want to be just like God made you, you ought to let 'em grow. Or why wear glasses or shave? Why wear a hearing-aid if you were born deaf? Why bother to have your teeth cavities fixed? Why wear clothes or shoes?"

Such talk sometimes reduced the poor sailor to confusion. Others, however, merely subsided into a stolid or angry silence.

Others who used religion as an excuse simply said, "My church is against it." I was prepared for that, too.

"There's nothing in the New Testament that prohibits tattoo-ing," I might say. "Now, if you're an Orthodox Jew, yes. There's a definite prohibition against marks on the body, and they have to be removed by a rabbi before burial"—and I would cite chapter and verse of Leviticus. "However," I would continue, "if you're a Christian, in the Book of Revelations in the New Testament, you will find this statement—" and here I would turn around a small standing sign so that they could read:

> And he [i.e., the Angel of the Word of God] hath on his ves-ture and on his thigh a name written: *King of Kings*, and *Lord of Lords*.
>
> —*Revelation 19. 18.*

If they were Christians their arguments often crumbled after that. But occasionally something amusing happened. A plump Jewish sailor wanted a tattoo and announced he was perfectly aware of the law about rabbinical removal. He got an anchor, a part of the design being a five-pointed star on each side of the anchor shaft. Would I please, he asked, make those into the six-pointed Stars of David. He felt that he had made a satisfactory compromise between his sailor's desire for a tattoo and his father's orthodoxy.

When my tattoo career began I grew quite interested in religious dicta concerning the "profession," and looked diligently through the writings of the Church fathers and the Bible itself—both Old and New Testaments—for some word on the subject.

There were several statements, ranging all the way from com-ment on the mark of Cain in the Old Testament to the Mark of the Beast in the New Testament. Some of them are here:

> *Genesis 4.15*: And the Lord said unto him, Therefore whoso-ever slayeth Cain, vengeance shall be taken on him sevenfold. And the Lord set a mark upon Cain, lest any finding him should kill him.

Here the mark seems to be "protective" so that Cain should not be killed for his crime, but suffer for a long time. This use of the mark may account for the general prohibition against all marks on the body, for the Jews; they would bear the associational stigma of the "mark of Cain."

> *Leviticus 19. 28:* **Ye shall not make any cuttings in your flesh for the dead, nor print any marks upon you: I am the Lord.**

These are the only two references in the Old Testament against tattooing which through exegesis and interpretation account for the Orthodox Jewish edict against tattoos. Note that these do not apply to Christians, coming as they do from the books of law, intended only for the Jews.

From the New Testament, however, come several about tattooing — or what might be interpreted as tattooing.

> *Galatians 6.17:* From henceforth let no man trouble me, for I bear in my body the marks of the Lord Jesus.

Here Saint Paul may indeed be speaking figuratively; there is no way of knowing. On the other hand, the context might very well denote the "protective" mark which kept Cain alive. Who can really tell? Has anyone a direct pipeline to the source, or must we all depend on the elaborate explanations of the scholars or priests or falwells?

> *Revelation 3.12:* Him that overcometh will I make a pillar in the temple of my God and he shall go no more out, and I will write upon him the name of my God, and the name of the city of my God, which is New Jerusalem, which cometh down out of heaven from my God; and *I will write upon him* my new name.
> [Italics sic]
> *Revelation 19.12:* [The angel of the Vision of the Word of God is described:] His eyes were as a flame of fire, and on his head were many crowns, and he had a name written, that no man knew, but he himself.

Then in *Revelation 19.18* occurred the lines that were used in my sign, but I had to explain what "vesture" meant to most of those boys. There were several other references, but the point has been made. Some refer to the Mark of the Beast, 666, which the Hells Angels adopted after a falwell denounced them.

* * * * *

A young man's buddies were often the best salesmen for a tattoo. They would urge him, badger him ("You ain't a man until you do," or "You ain't got a hair in yer ass unless you do") and often override his excuses and objections. I never permitted myself to "sell" a customer on the idea of getting one. Many of the arcade jaggers used the hard-sell method. Sometimes they even pulled a young man into their shops by the arm, plunked him down in the chair and said something like: "I've got just the tattoo for you, young feller." I would simply greet a person who came into the shop, and then let him look. If he asked "What's a good tattoo for me?" I would explain that only he could decide that. "If you pick out two designs I can tell you which is the better one, but that's all. I don't know what your attitudes and interests are."

With this technique I salved my conscience a bit, because I knew how the tattoos would look in twenty years, how the colors would fade and blur as the ink sank down into the skin and diffused into the neighbor cells. And when the person no longer wanted it, I had no desire to be blamed for talking him into getting it. If such a feeling leads anyone to conclude that I should not have been in the business if I felt that way about it, all I can hide behind is the weasel-rationalization that "if I don't put it on, someone else will."

Besides, it was fun. I was having the most enjoyable time of my life, things were happening that I found incredible or fascinating, and I was making money. Greed takes nearly all businessmen into the land of compromise with morality and ethics.

This troublesome conscience of mine kept me silent when a prospect was wandering around the room, but it also earned me a reputation for fair dealing, and it was responsible for compliments such as "Chee, I like to come in here. You don't grab me and try to sell me sumpin like the other guys do."

My conscience took other forms, too. Sometimes I talked a young man out of getting a tattoo if he were uncertain about wanting one. If he inquired about how to get it off, he was advised that if he were worried about removal, it would be much better not to have it in the first place. And very often he left, walking out the door with a large dollar sign glimmering on his back . . . Finally, although I find it difficult to believe after thirty years, from time to time I actually refused to tattoo a young man, either because I knew that he would regret it, or because he was too damned handsome to spoil his body with a tattoo. Such a statement, born of my particular sexual orientation, can be understood only by others similarly constructed.

Old Randy in the arcade used to scold me all the time for this non-salesmanship, as he considered it. "You'd oughta say to 'em, right when they first come in, 'Wanta tattoo, sonny?' You ain't never gonna get no business doin' the way you do, jus' settin' and watchin' 'em look." But the volume of business during the time when I was alone in the shop proved Randy to be very wrong indeed.

The only selling technique used was hardly that at all, but more a reassuring joke, a part of the patter. *After* a boy had decided on a design which was going to have a girl's name in the banner, he might still be unsure and say something like: "My girl will give me hell for this." I would then express a kind of comfort to him: "Ah – she'll really love it. She'll throw her arms around your neck and say 'Oh, Jimmy, you really DO love me after all!'"

In fact, my conscience sometimes caused me to lean over backwards the wrong way. A person would often be in the place for thirty minutes to an hour just silently looking at the designs. I found this to be a time wasting nuisance, since sometimes his remarks would indicate he was not looking at the flash for a design, but was trying to decide whether to get one. At such moments, patience wearing thin, I might say: "My boy, a tattoo shop is *not* a place to decide if you want one; it's a place you come to *after* you decide you want one. Why don't you go home now and think about it a while longer and then come back and pick one – *if* you decide to get one." And often the young man would leave – and once again I would see the dollar sign fading on his back as he went out the door. But in a way it was worth it, just as I deliberately used to "lend" a tiresome hanger-on a buck, knowing well that he would never return to repay me.

One thing about the browsers came to irritate me a lot. When someone came in merely to look, with no idea of getting a tattoo, he could usually not find an excuse to leave. Then he would ask: "How long do you keep open?" with an inflection that suggested he would be back before I closed. Or he might say "I'll be back tomorrow," or "I'll be back soon." Nine times out of ten I never saw him again; if he did return, my surprise was great. In California I eventually made a little sign to tack on the door: "You don't have to say 'I'll be back' — just 'Goodbye' will do."

In the classroom I had never been noted for an over-abundance of patience. In fact, I had always been quick to express myself sardonically when confronted with stupidity, non-preparation, or the inability to answer simple questions. But there was one thing that tattooing compelled me to learn —

To be patient, and to wait.

PART IX

Masters, Methods, and Maladies

It would be unwise to attempt any kind of evaluation of present day tattoo artists, just as it would be impossible to try to number them. Mentioning names would be an invitation to disaster. In this jealous, backbiting, cut-throat world slighting anyone by omitting names might result in an attempt on the part of the omitted ones to get their revenge somehow — either by malice, gossip, or some more tangible method.

Having said this, I nonetheless intend later in this section to speak of a few tattoo artists whom I consider to be the best at work in this country. My protection against possible retaliation lies in the fact that I abandoned the racket twenty years ago, and consider myself reasonably armored against any kind of retaliation. And just why did I abandon this seductive, erotic, and lucrative life? Well, my location in Oakland was not in the best possible area in that not very attractive city [there was no there there, to quote Ms. Stein], and I was strong-armed and robbed three times by our black brothers. To avoid a fourth time — and the possible knife or bullet (which sent an old neighboring pawnbroker to a premature rendezvous with Yahweh) I closed the shop in 1970, leaving no trace whatsoever of Philyppe Sparrow.

There are among the new breed of tattoo artists many undoubtedly skillful practitioners, both of the younger generation in their thirties, and the middle generation in the forties and fifties. The very old generation has mostly died by now — the people who became legendary in their own time: Charlie Wagner, Percy Waters, Amund Dietzel, Bert Grimm, and a few others.

Some of the old artists, now dead, did not do work that would be satisfactory by modern standards. They used outline machines that were too thick and heavy, making delicate fine-line work impossible. Their small stuff "closed up"—that is, the slight spreading of the outline that occurs in every tattoo was very marked in their work. A name, for example, in which the letters were adequately spaced when first put on, might in three years' time become unreadable. The letters "n" and "m" would close together; the loops in the "a" and "e" would come to look like "o." Many of the old boys never really learned how to tattoo well during the early years of their experience, and went on to the ends of their lives doing second-rate work, botched, imperfectly shaded, and excessively heavy.

In the ballet world, when by general agreement a prima ballerina receives the ultimate honor, the title *assoluta*, her absolute perfection is universally recognized. Such a term might be applied to Amund Dietzel of Milwaukee. The purity and assurance of his line, the supreme and absolute confidence with which he created his tattoos, could be recognized even by a lay observer. The designs which he created had a certain old-fashioned charm—his Navy girls were rosy-cheeked and full-faced, ladies of the early 1900s, looking with a kind of nostalgic attractiveness out on a world which had outpaced them and moved on to more modern allures.

"Dietz" was in a sense my teacher, and I learned more from him about tattooing than from any other person. He looked rather like a benign university professor, small, in his seventies when I first met him, with blond white hair that showed his Scandinavian ancestry. He gave an impression of confidence and contentment, as if he taught something undisturbing like Greek or Anglo-Saxon. It was the small nervous enthusiast Larry who first took me to see him, and I did not then know with what distrust Dietzel would view me for appearing under the aegis of Larry, whom he loathed.

When we entered his shop he was initially crusty with Larry, and some of his spininess spilled in my direction. But as he went on working on the design that Larry wanted, the first grouchiness evaporated, and by the end of an hour he was quite pleasant. Both Larry and I stayed in the shop for several hours, watching as Dietzel worked on other customers, and by the end of that time I had learned more about tattooing than I had known until then.

That first visit marked the beginning of a long and enjoyable friendship. Dietz became a kind of ideal for me. True, like all of us, he had his bad days when he was grumpy, impatient, and crotchety; and you learned not to irritate him or cross him when his patience was thin. He helped me with many minor problems in tattooing, taught me about the best colors, and sold me some excellent tattoo machines—medium heavy-duty ones. The *extra*-heavy duty machines—much longer lasting—he kept for himself. "You've got to look out for number one," he said, grinning.

It was easy to identify a Dietzel tattoo. His line-work was thin and superb; his shading and coloring surpassed even his line. The colors stayed brilliant for years. He had some of the jealousy which besets every tattooist, but his work was so far superior to any other that he needn't have had any qualms at all. For many years he had ruled as absolute master of tattooing in Milwaukee. His prices were low and he worked like the wind—very fast. If a competitor set up shop in Milwaukee, Dietz lowered his prices even more. The sailors flocked to him; his word-of-mouth reputation was widespread. In the course of his long career he became a very wealthy man, but he never stopped to spend his money until a local ordinance closed tattooing on "moral" grounds in Milwaukee in June, 1967. Like the rest of us, the virus of tattooing had got into his blood. In his last two years, when his eyes began to blur he worked with an assistant; but until that time his finished product surpassed that of all other tattooists. With justifiable vanity he used to chortle, "I can still tattoo rings around the best of 'em."

Dietz had a line on his business cards that said "50 + years' experience," changing the figure as each year passed. It was always a practice among lesser artists to claim "forty years' experience" even if they were just beginners only thirty years old. In the last printing of cards for my Chicago shop, I added a line "146 years' experience" as a wry joke. Proving that the clientele could barely read, in the nine months following the printing of that line only two persons called me on what was the most obvious of fabrications. Perhaps it was not really obvious to them; a sailor once said, "Chee, I can't tell the age of anyone over nineteen."

Dietz undoubtedly was the best Old Master—but he has now passed from the scene, and it must be admitted that he stayed a little too long. He should have stopped when his eyes failed, but he didn't.

In my opinion the two best tattoo artists in the United States today are Don Ed Hardy, working in his Realistic Studio in San Francisco, and Cliff Raven, located in Los Angeles on the Strip. Admittedly I have not seen the work of many other tattooists who have been born to blush unseen, and neither is it to be denied that I had some small hand in starting both of the tattooists just named on their careers, yet I feel that I can honestly and objectively call them the best of all the American artists.

They are both extremely careful workmen, using tightly controlled thin but stable outlines, and great varieties of pigments and colors. Both of them can insert their brilliant pigments into the skin without scarring; and both can make sure that the colors are laid in properly so that they remain. As designers it would be difficult to say that one is better than the other. Perhaps Hardy excels in Oriental designs, whereas Raven succeeds in outré originality. Both of them are meticulous in matters of sanitation and antisepsis, unlike several pretenders who use their autoclaves as glove compartments, to store cigarettes instead of sterilize equipment. Neither has sought publicity at the expense of good work, but has contented himself with a reputation solidly earned by word-of-mouth based exclusively on the quality of work done, instead of the number of celebrities tattooed, in the way that some popular tattooists have created their undeserved "glamour."

*   *   *   *   *

There is no reason to try to include here a manual on the art of tattooing, but a general exposition of the process is within bounds.

The skin is first shaved. For this many old-time jaggers used tincture of green soap and a straight-edged razor. Early on I discarded this wicked and terrifying implement because of its psychological effect on the customer. Set a young man down for his first tattoo, his first step into a strange experience, and then unsheathe and unfold a glittering blade in front of him. His fright increases to the point where he sometimes faints at once. He is already frightened enough by the rumors he has heard of the fearful pain — and by the taunts and remarks of his friends who have come to watch his "deflowering." Instead of the razor, I used a good surgical electric clipper, and found this did much to remove the initial terror, although the clipper somewhat diminished the rite-of-passage aspect.

After the skin is shaved, it is sterilized either with zephiran chloride or 70° alcohol. Then it is lightly greased with carbolated vaseline. One takes the template of the design, which we mistakenly call a stencil, and rubs a bit of pure carbon dust over the outline. These templates we make ourselves, tracing the designs with a needle-point held in a chuck, on acetate thick enough to form a small powder-catching burr. Then the template is pressed against the vaselined skin, leaving an imprint.

Some tattooists brag about being "free-hand" artists, and con their customers into thinking this is a superior method. This is not true. If a tattooist puts on a design while holding the skin taut, disaster occurs. The design may look all right while the skin is stretched tight, but when it is released the "free-hand" tattoo warps out of shape, either by multiple irregularities or by narrowing itself into a thin El Greco caricature.

Great care must be taken in the placing of the carbon design, and due regard given to the area of the body whereon the tattoo is made. If someone wants a design on the groin area, for example, he should be lying on a bench with knees drawn up so that the imprint is not made on stretched skin. Otherwise it will shrink together when he stands up. Similar care should be taken with a deltoid or pectoral placement.

Once the outline is on the skin, the artist traces it with what is called an outliner. The needles in this are like a fine writing point; there are from three to five bunched together and soldered to a needle-bar, which moves rapidly up and down between two and three thousand times a minute. Frequent dippings into the color supply are necessary. The needles are not hollow like hypodermics. The ink merely lies between them; the adhesion is a natural one. The fewer needles used, the finer the outline, and the less spreading of ink occurs later. A group of five, tightly bunched, usually gives the most pleasing and permanent results.

In my own mind I categorized skin in eight types, number one being thin, fine, and delicate as a rose-leaf—very easy to tattoo; the ink seemed almost to sink in by gravity. Type eight I thought of as "old elephant hide"—thick and tough, demanding repeated cross-ings with the wide shader needle to get the ink to stay in. There was one certain body type, rather plump and heavy with very light white skin, which was both my despair and joy. The colors went in very easily and stayed brighter longer than they did on less delicate skins. The "despair" rose from the fact that on such skin the slight-est imperfection, or any wavering of the outline showed with star-tling clarity.

One always had to work with the greatest care. It was flattering to hear a bystander once remark: "That Sparrow, he's the gahdamned-est perfectionist I ever saw." I took as many pains with a dollar tattoo as with a twenty-dollar one; excellent work brought other customers into the shop, but the sloppy work of Randy or Jake earned for them advertisements like: "For crissakes, don't go there; you'll be fucked up and you gotta wear it for the rest of your life."

The actual pigments used in tattooing were all of metallic rather than organic base. They arrived as dry colors, ranging from a light and fluffy green of which a pound filled a two pound coffee can, whereas a pound of red—because of its heavy specific gravity [mer-cury]—filled only a small-sized envelope. The colors were moist-ened with 190° grain alcohol [grain neutral spirits] until they be-came a thick paste. Too thick will not work; too thin will not leave enough residual color behind. Each pigment and color has its own consistency, a thing that tattooists have to learn by trial. Less thick is the black: a concentrated black India ink, imported from Ger-many, which contained certain additives that seemed to keep the outlines from early spreading.

The colors should be kept in capped squeeze-bottles, and a few drops put into individual heavy plastic capsules, of the type com-monly used to contain bull sperm. Today, in the age of hepatitis, syphilis, and AIDS, the careful customer should note the following:

If you should see that a tattoo artist uses small two-ounce jars for his pigments, and repeatedly dips his needles into them—please run like hell, for this inept and tragically dangerous operator is capable of transmitting any number of modern diseases, and is a greater threat than the junkie who shares his needle with other addicts!

Such a tattooist is obviously guilty of contaminating all his pigments, and his needles pass on any virus a previous customer has left behind.

The colored pigments are inserted within the black outline, which seems to provide a holding effect; without it, the colors are less permanent. For the colors, a different type of needle called a shader is used; it is usually eight needles wide. The shader is not as painful as the outliner, for the striking force is diminished — spread out — by the greater width. The pigments must be used in sequence from dark to light, because a drop of black spattered on the red, for example, while the tattoo is "open," will sink in and discolor the red. Many tattooists, interested more in money than art, refuse to shade with black; their finished work looks like that in a kindergarten coloring book. Shading is the secret of good tattooing; it gives rotundity and body to the design. Without it a four-petaled flower may look like a propeller on a boat, or a sphere like a mere filled-in circle.

Each pigment should have its own needle; otherwise all the colors turn muddy, because the instruments cannot be sufficiently cleaned out and sterilized between pigments. First black, then green or blue, then red, yellow, and perhaps white.

Proper sterilizing and bandaging finish the tattoo, and the customer should be again cautioned about keeping it as dry as possible.

What to charge? Ah, that's impossible to say. In the 1950s prices were a fifth of what they are today, when many artists will not wet a needle for less than twenty or thirty dollars, and the best workers make $150 or more an hour. In the '50s I was almost embarrassed to ask for $20 an hour. Do not pity the "poor tattoo artist." He is secure, confident, and reasonably wealthy, owning condominiums and real estate and possibly a Swiss bank account. When you consider that the actual cost of a tattoo — including rent, gas, heat, and light — is about fifty cents for a fifteen minute one, for which he charges forty dollars today, you will begin to understand why most successful tattoo artists are expert in "poor-mouthing" their profession. You can never tell when one of Uncle Sugar's spies is lurking behind the door, waiting to pounce. And the large bills go into the left pocket, the fives and tens into the right. He will never make as much as fast as a crack cocaine dealer, but he's right up there with the best professionals.

My prices in the 1950s and 1960s were 40 to 60% lower than those of my competitors. Consequently it was extraordinarily irritating to have a fuzzy-cheeked youth come into my shop and say:

"Chee, your prices are high!"

To this I developed a standard response. "Well, you have to look on it as a sort of lifetime investment. If the tattoo costs five dollars and you're good for fifty years more, then that would make it cost about ten cents a year. Not very much."

Their reply was usually standard, too. "Hell, I ain't gonna make it even to thirty."

Mortido. Death-wish. The young are always astonished as the years go on, faster and faster. He reaches thirty-five, forty—without having died as early as he thought. "Live fast, die young, and be a good-lookin' corpse" is a motto hardly ever realized, but age cannot ever convince youth of this.

"How long do they really last?" was sometimes a second query.

"For life and six months." And I would point to the small plastic skeleton holding that sign. "And then the worms take over."

The short laugh that dismissed my statement showed me that the young were really not capable of extending their vision more than two weeks beyond the present moment.

* * * * *

The question of diseases transmissible by tattoo needles is a serious one for every ethical tattoo artist. If he knows anything about the subject at all, he realizes that he must be very careful about his procedures.

The ailments which may be transmitted by the tattoo needle are several. If they were to be listed in degree of seriousness, the first would undoubtedly be AIDS, acquired immuno-deficiency syndrome; the second, hepatitis; the third, syphilis; the fourth, staphylococcal infections; and the fifth, warts.

AIDS is a relatively "new" disease so far as is known; we did not have to worry about it in the 1950s and 1960s. In 1990 the human immuno-deficiency virus [HIV], is, alas, all too familiar.

It is the most fatal of all blood-transmissible viruses. Other body substances such as tears, saliva, and semen need not be of great concern to the tattooist. But blood is the great danger, and the modern tattooist should wear rubber gloves, not only to safeguard himself but his customers as well. Clorox and alcohol are the preferred viricides for HIV; all equipment should be autoclaved or subjected to sterilization by clorox. Needle-pricks can be fatal if they carry the HIV virus. Black fingernails are the sign of a dangerous ungloved tattoo artist; avoid him as you would the plague.

But we did have to worry about hepatitis in the 1950s and 1960s, or "yellow jaundice" as it was popularly called then — a really serious ailment confronting the tattoo artist. Technically it was not the hepatitis A virus [HAV] which could be spread by eating contaminated shellfish, or water or foodborne contaminants, but rather HB-Virus, transmitted by needles from a worldwide reservoir provided by chronic carriers. Vaccination against HBV today gives an almost universal anti-HBs response in normal recipients, but autoclaving protects the tattoo customer against HBV, syphilis, and warts.

It was always my practice to ask each customer if he had had hepatitis, but never to depend on his answer, taking for granted the fact that he had had it, as well as syphilis and warts. Zephiran chloride and the autoclave had taken care of all the ailments of the 1950s and 1960s. I am personally glad that I ended my tattooing career in 1970; I would not for anything in the world be tattooing in this day of AIDS. The time of gravest danger lies ahead for both the customer and the tattooist, who needs whatever advice and help a doctor can give him in setting up the system of antisepsis for his shop.

PART X

Art and the Tattoo

Lycurgus once stated a universal truth when he said that every man wants to leave behind a monument by which he would be remembered. With Lycurgus it was the beauty of his laws; with the ordinary man, his children perpetuate his name and memory. With a novelist or poet, the writings suffice. Gertrude Stein once remarked that she would be happy if a reading public returned to her writings in twenty-year waves.

Pity the poor tattoo artist. His is certainly a mayfly art, perhaps the least enduring of all, save for the improvisations of Arabian music. The canvas he works on is the human skin, and his "art" is frequently covered by clothing. Even if it is visible, its life is limited by the life of the customer, unless an Ilse Koch should make a lampshade of his skin. Perhaps its life is even less than that, for the tattoo does not retain its brightness for a longer period than fifteen or twenty years. It fades; the black takes on a bluish cast as the color sinks into the skin, lower and lower, diffusing into the neighboring cells. Contrary to the general folkloristic belief, a tattoo does not grow upwards and out. Two French doctors, making a post-mortem of a tattooed man, found traces of the black ink of an old tattoo deep on the bone of his forearm.

Certainly the transience of a tattoo undermines the permanency of the "monument" which the tattoo artist leaves behind himself. There is an amusing but disheartening story about the wife of a west coast tattooist, herself accomplished in the craft. She was once engaged in completely covering a male customer, having worked on him for nearly three years. She was within four hours of completing the lengthy project when the police descended on her shop and arrested the male customer on a charge of murder, took him to San

Quentin and in due time escorted him to the gas chamber. It nearly unraveled the lady artist and frustrated her so much that she was unable to tattoo again for quite a while.

There is not much creativity nor originality among tattoo artists as a whole. Obviously, someone at some time had to create the designs first, and there are few talented designers in the field. But the majority of tattoo artists have never had any art training. Most of them are content to borrow or steal the designs of others, and the technique of the template makes it easy for even the least-skilled hack to put on a design, no matter how crudely. All he needs is to get a picture of the right size.

Up until the 1930s any observer of tattoo "flash" was struck with the similarity of the faces of the ladies. All of them had a decidedly Semitic cast to the nose and face — which could be traced back to a tattoo artist who worked in Cleveland, Ohio — a man who had created hundreds of designs. He called himself Lew-the-Jew, and his busts and faces were copied for years, and are still used by the least talented jaggers.

It was Lew-the-Jew who got tattooing declared illegal in Ohio, save for the few cases where a tattooist has been able to persuade the local chief of police to give him a permit to operate. Lew had tattooed a sixteen-year-old boy, and the boy's mother — with the parish priest — had gone to Lew to complain. As the priest looked at the flash, he noticed on one card that a head of Jesus Christ was placed next to a nearly naked Hawaiian dancing girl. He spoke to Lew, saying that he thought Lew might find a better place for Our Lord. But Lew was drunk as usual, and said with an expansive gesture: "Why not there? It's as good a place as any for the old sonofabitch."

Bang! Within twenty-four hours the city of Cleveland passed an ordinance against tattooing, which was later extended to become a state law with the proviso of local option.

Many young men have come into the shop to say: "I want a good original tattoo, sumpin no one else's got." When I showed them my collection of original designs, they would turn vague and unhappy. "Naw, that's *too* different," they might say, and then end by getting a panther or a skunk or eagle.

The clientele was not notable for its originality. A tattoo to them ought to "look like a tattoo," which was to say that it had to *conform* to their idea of all tattoos. It had to be like something which they had seen before on someone. The designs, therefore, had to be completely stylized. It was not enough for a panther to look photographically like a panther. Indeed, the customer demanded that it look like his *idea* of what a panther should be, or like the one on his buddy's arm. Any resemblance to the real thing should be purely coincidental. I once put on my flash the design of a human heart, copied from an anatomy book, aorta and arteries and all, and stuck an arrow through it—to replace the stylized red heart and arrow usual on valentine cards. In eight years only two persons were cynical and/or whimsical enough to get it.

Once in a while there were intelligent customers who really knew what they wanted. A young man said he wanted a Latin motto inscribed around and above a small red heart. The motto he had chosen was that of the Prioress in Chaucer's Prologue to the *Canterbury Tales*: Amor vincit omnia—love conquers all. Such an original request caused me to spend quite a little time designing the tattoo, with scrollwork surrounding it, so that it looked like the brooch the Prioress wore, or like a small illumination in a medieval manuscript. To top things, we quoted alternating lines from the Prologue's introduction to each other. Fortunately, no one else was in the shop at the time, to hear us go sing-songing through "Whan that Aprille with his shoures soote . . ."

Tattooing is perhaps one of the last genuine folk-arts in the United States. Many of the designs have a certain primitive charm. Two of the standard ones, long-lived in popularity, were the black panther crawling up the arm, and the small skunk holding a flower, usually called "Lil Stinker."

No one can say with whom the black panther originated. Several of the old timers have claimed to have designed it first, but its origin is not known. Usually the panther is seen slanted and supposedly crawling up the arm, its head turned in profile and its tail given a graceful arc. It is a difficult design to put on effectively. Most of the jaggers and hacks make no attempt to create shading to show the muscle-structure of the beast, but simply make it into a black silhouette. If the job is bungled, nothing can be done to repair it, for black is the dominant color and shows through all other pigments.

A botched panther is there to stay, and no improvement of it is possible.

Amund Dietzel of Milwaukee laid claim to having invented the "Lil Stinker" skunk, and perhaps he did—or got the idea from Disney. The little skunk in all its thousand variant forms has remained consistently popular for the longest time of any of the comic tattoos. Most boys between eighteen and twenty [in the 1950s] thought it cute; just what they may think of it when they are forty is hard to say.

The comic tattoos come and go, many of them "flash-in-the-pan" ones, with a life no longer than a popular song. After six months the customer is tired of it and wants it covered. "Popeye" was such a one, and for several years the little scowling red devil called "Hot Stuff," holding a pitchfork and wearing a diaper, was another. Requests to have it covered began about six weeks after placement. The Playboy bunny also amused the young men for a while and made them feel adult; but what their reactions to it may be when they reach middle-age is another matter.

There were certain standard designs which were never complained of; these seemed to remain emotionally satisfying to the wearer no matter what his age. I never heard anyone say that he wanted a rose or an eagle covered. Most of the old Navy designs seemed to satisfy the wearers, perhaps for sentimental reasons or as a remembrance of the good old days and adventures experienced on the duty rack.

On the other hand, all too many of the young men get their girl's name artistically inscribed on their arm—"real fancy lettering, now." They usually regret it. They are warned that things may change, but every young man believes that a situation which exists now is going to go on forever. He joins the army or navy, gets a "Dear John" letter, and then wants her name covered with flowers, so that she is buried forever beneath the roses.

A sailor once brought in a photograph of his girl and wanted me to translate it into a tattoo for his arm. He returned two days later after I had made the design and got the tattoo. A week later he returned.

"Phil," he said, "gahdamn it, I got a Dear John letter this morning. Can you cover up this tattoo?"

"Not possible," I said, "you'll have to wait until it heals completely. Come back in a month."

"Cheez," he wailed, "I can't look at it that long! Can't you at least do sumpin with it?"

"Like what?" I said.

"Oh, put a big handlebar mustache on her face," he said, "like you see on signboards."

That's what we did. The story appeared in local newspapers.

How does one select a good tattoo artist from the jungle of jaggers and hacks? A warning has already been given about what to consider if you want to avoid unsanitary workers—the size of the pigment jars. But picking an *accomplished* artist instead of a hack who knows nothing beyond his stencils is difficult. If it is possible to see a tattooist's healed and finished work, you can judge if you like it. If you can watch the guy working, look at the freshly finished design. Has a fine-line outline been used, or one that is too thick? Are the colors bright? Do they seem to be well put into the skin or are there lighter patches here and there? Does the color come exactly up to the black of the outline? Or does it lap over? Is the overall effect pleasing, or cramped or stringy?

You cannot always depend on the number of customers in a shop as an indicator of the artist's skill. Perhaps the best artist has an obscure location, or perhaps the worst has prices that are too high. It pays to shop around a bit, to watch and observe. After all, the tattoo will be with you the rest of your life. It is decidedly unwise to think that one tattooist is as good as another.

And never, never allow a tattoo artist to start work on you if you see that he is drunk, or smell liquor on him. You will have a long time to regret it if you sit in his chair.

PART XI

The Tattooist and His World

Someone once said that to be a tattoo artist you needed the patience of Job, the *equanimitas* of Sir William Osler, and the capabilities of a draftsman. Certainly this is true, but it hardly goes far enough. A tattoo artist has to be a kind of jack-of-all-trades. He must in turn be a psychologist, a con-man, an electrician. He must be a jeweler, to work with fine small parts and to repair his needles; a kind of Florence Nightingale or medico when the boys get woozy; an accountant, to keep his books — if any; an astute public relations man, to handle the little old ladies and the falwell cranks; a creative artist, to make the new designs; an accomplished draftsman, to produce an attractive flash; a dermatologist, to recognize skin characteristics and ailments; a priest, to hear the confessions and not be shocked; a semanticist, to control the drunks who arrive with either a chip on the shoulder or a wild hair in the nose; and sometimes a bouncer, if words fail to work. He must even be a graphologist, to determine if the "permission" notes were written by Mom or sonny-boy. And then finally, he must be his own janitor, window-washer, display advertiser, and general factotum.

The irritant factors in a tattoo artist's life are numerous and intense. He is continually faced with an unending barrage of questions from both customers and onlookers. He knows quite well that many of the questions are asked by persons who have no desire at the moment to get a tattoo. But there is always the old adage that you can catch more flies with honey than vinegar, and always the chance that some day the questioner might return for a tattoo. And so, over and over, the same old questions must be answered until the process becomes automatic. After a few years you no longer listened: the query was registered, and somewhere in the mysterious computer of the brain the relays clicked and closed, and out of the mouth came the proper response. Only occasionally was one so jolted by a bizarre question that the brain came alive to answer the question with a response that demanded some thought.

And the questions? Based mostly on folklore or ignorance —

Does it hurt? How long does it take? What's the danger of infection? Can they be removed? Howja do it — with goat's milk? Pregnant mare's piss? Lemon juice? Clorox? Can't you cover 'em with flesh color? Chee, can the eyeball be tattooed? How long did your chest-piece take? All in one settin'? How much did it cost? Who did it? How old is it? You got any others? How deep do the needles go? How many needles in those machines? What kind of current do you use? How many times they go a minute? What're the handcuffs for? Is that skull real? Did you put the dagger through it? Is that the way he got killed? Is it a man's or woman's? How come you're not covered all over like the other tattooers? Howja get into this racket? You got any other sidelines? You gotta be an artist to do this? You make your own designs? Stencils? Howja make the stencils? You gotta head in here? What is that black powder? How long were you an apprentice? Are there any schools for this? Howja learn it? What'd you practice on? Who was your teacher? Are those colors Indian ink? Vegetable dyes? What dyuh mean — metallic? What-dyuh mix 'em with? How do you sterilize 'em? What's an autoclave? Where do you get new needles? How much they cost? What do the colors cost? Can I use the john? How do you make the needles? Who makes your designs? What's in that wash water? Who makes your stencils? What's a template? What's that furrin' language mean in the can? How long does a tattoo last? Djever tattoo anybody all over? Do you tattoo women? Where? How many people you covered? Even their dongs? Any pussies? How many cocks you tattooed? What's that you're puttin' on me now? What's zephiran chloride? What's benzalkonium chloride? How do I take care of it? How many times I wash it? How come no vaseline? Kin I go swimmin' with it? Why not? How long does it take to heal? Where'd you get the swords? Why does that clock run backwards? Did you draw all these designs? What dyuh mean — "flash?" What's the biggest tattoo you got in the shop? What's the most you ever charged for a tattoo? What's the longest time it ever took to put one on? Got any tattoos for a dollar? Any cheaper than that? Kin I use the john? Do you take tattoos off? How's that done? Didja hear the one about the guy with a dot on his dong?

Multiply such questions by about a hundred and fifty thousand customers, allowing about ten questions a person, and you begin to have an idea of the kind of patience required of the tattoo artist. Not all of us were able to maintain a high degree of this virtue. The growling crotchety tattooists greatly outnumbered those with Job's forbearance.

During the early days in Chicago until I developed my protective armor-plate against queries, I lettered a "price list" for them as a gag. Unfortunately, all too many visitors to the shop took it seriously. Here it is:

1. For using the shop as a meeting place.....................50¢
2. For giving advice to the lovelorn.........................$1.00
3. For listening to tales of woe.................................75
4. For 1/2 hour of good stimulating talk......................1.00
5. For silly questions about tattooing . . . each.................35
6. For use of can without getting tattoo........................25
7. For making change for parking meters......................50
8. For giving directions...1.00
9. For listening to other tattooers' bullshit....................2.50
10. For talking about women I've tattooed.......................40
11. For listening to jokes about tattooed dongs.................3.50
12. For reading comic books without getting tattooed...........50
13. For talking about techniques of tattooing...................1.50
14. For cheering people up..1.25
15. For "lending" people a buck..................................3.00
16. For answering questions about the money I make........4.00
17. For listening to ordinary garden-type bullshit..............1.00
18. For explaining how tattoos are removed....................1.50
19. For hearing "I'm bleeding like a stuck pig"...............1.00
20. For miscellaneous irritation..................................2.00

This was by no means the entire list of grievances, but it conveys an idea of the nature and number of the annoyances. Few of the customers could read more than the first line, and if I pointed to a certain number might manage to stumble through it.

There was one phrase that bugged me extremely. I had always hated to hear it said by a person on the telephone. It was: "I'll let you go now . . ." and it always prompted me to make a heavily sarcastic remark about masters and slaves. In the tattoo shop it was used in such remarks as "I'll let you put a tattoo on me when I come back tomorrow," or "I'll let you work it over," or "I'll let you finish it," or "I'll let you put the color back in." With the inflection invariably given the phrase, it sounded as if they were giving some kind of sexual permission, and it irritated me beyond all reason. I would put one elbow on my knee and lean forward and say something like: "Well, I'll tell you, bud, I'm just a-dyin' for the great and honorable privilege of you lettin' me put a tattoo on you, and all it'll take will be for me to be in the right mood and you to have enough money in your pocket, and then if you're not drunk and can sit still and take it, maybe I'll let you beg me to work on you."

My shop in Chicago was so arranged that I could clearly hear what people said outside the door, but because of the street noises they could not hear what went on inside. Some of the remarks made outside would blister a less sensitive ear. It was irritating to hear some Ivy League type say to his exquisitely coiffed and dressed female something like:

"Let's go in and look at the place. We'll kid the old bum around and pretend we want a tattoo."

When they entered, smirking, I would beat them to the insult. "Ah, slummers!" I would say in a loud tone. "Come down to see how the other half lives, huh?"

This gave them momentary pause and set up a certain confusion. I would plunge ahead, pressing the advantage. "Well, I have a little nugget of news for you, kiddies. We live a lot better than you think."

After such a greeting they generally did not stay long, and some of them retired in total defeat.

The world of tattoo artists is full of very odd characters, granted. They are a jealous and independent lot. A question often asked in the shop by those unaware of the treacherous undercurrents and byzantine workings of such a world was: "Do you guys have a union?"

Such a question always amused me. To think there could be any common basis of agreement or co-operation established among such a crew of cut-throat operators, jealous "artists," and fiercely independent artisans would be as impossible as trying to get all American doctors to charge only twenty-five dollars for an appendectomy. In the tattoo jungle there could never be any trust established among them. Each is a little world to himself, convinced he is the best of all, that his techniques outshine all others, his machines are the most efficient, his flash the absolute best, and his work the most enduring, colorful, and effective.

Attempts have been made from time to time to form loose associations or clubs of tattoo artists. They have generally been short-lived. There is usually an annual convention, where both artists and tattoo buffs congregate for the purpose of showing off their body work, exchanging gossip, and getting drunk or laid. Not much is accomplished, but it is a pleasure for the exhibitionists and balm for the egos, and everyone has as much fun as at any grouping of Kiwanians or Rotarians, and undoubtedly more sport than at conventions of falwells. Mimeographed announcements sometimes arrive irregularly from mayfly organizations that briefly thrive and then are seen no more. Usually the publications are pointless miscellanies of old information and older photos, sometimes merely perpetuating many of the ancient errors regarding tattooing. One or two efforts by more intelligent persons have appeared, excellently illustrated on good coated stock, with articles written by intelligent and authoritative researchers. Some of these are surveyed in the appendices following the text.

PART XII

The Vanishing Art . . .?

One hot summer afternoon I was sitting peacefully in the shop, soldering some needles, when an apparition opened the door and held it wide. It was a Little Old Lady about five feet tall, dressed outlandishly in a mustard-colored coat and carrying a folded flowered umbrella and a net shopping bag. On her head was a straw hat with a flat brim, crowned with a profusion of purple fruits and orange flowers.

She screamed at me in a high cracked vicious old voice, "Ye're no damn good! The whole lot of ye's crooks and hoodlums!" she shrieked. "Ye've never done an honest day's work in yer whole life! If I had my way, ye'd all be closed up tight!"

With that she let the door fly shut and was on her way, leaving me speechless. After she had gone I thought of the many things I might have said to her, most of them obscene. But her reaction was typical of the nosey do-gooders, the falwells with their crazed smiles, who occasionally either by anonymous letter or phone call made life unhappy.

The Little Old Lady was symptomatic of an underwave of puritanism which exists in the United States—and the world, for that matter. She was a single unit of a very large portion of the population, and her method of expressing her displeasure was direct and straightforward; her life and conduct, her morals and thinking, were all guided by the biblical code. For those like her, tattooing is a barbarous remnant of a primitive and uncivilized—yes, wicked and sinful way of life. The puritan mind she represented feels vaguely that there is something *wrong* with tattooing, and they disapprove of it emotionally. If you could find any of them intelligent enough to discuss it, you would uncover the subterranean current of patristic puritanism and hypocrisy, which exist so noticeably in the last half of the twentieth century—two legs of the three-legged stool on which this country is balanced.

There have been throughout history great swings of a pendulum between restrictiveness and permissiveness in society. Within these great swings occur numerous small alternations of the same kind, but shorter in time-span and more noticeable than the large ones. In 1954 G. Rattray Taylor, a British psychohistorian, published a fascinating work entitled *Sex in History*, a subject too often omitted from the text-books.

One of his most interesting comparisons is that of the differences between the patristic [restrictive] and the matristic [permissive] societies. The patristic is more restrictive in all things, considering women inferior and limiting their freedom; prizing chastity more than welfare; inhibited, distrustful of all forms of research and inquiry; deeply fearing homosexuality, gender confusion through dress, and pleasure of all kinds; politically conservative and authoritarian; and against all innovation. The matristic society—which would seem by the 1980s to be in the process of being abandoned— stood for the opposites in most areas: a permissive attitude towards sex; freedom for women (who were accorded high status); welfare valued more than chastity; democratic and revolutionary viewpoints with no distrust of research; spontaneity and exhibition; a deep fear of incest; sexual differences minimized; and hedonism and pleasure welcomed.

It is not necessary to draw conclusions at this point; they are more than evident. Anyone who reads or listens to the news can understand what the future of tattooing might be in a patristic society. The matristic 1960s were one thing; the 1980s were another. One hesitates to look deeply into the 1990s, and the next century may be too bleak for even the most superficial glance to be endured.

In general, tattoo artists have in the past been what the British might call a "scurvy lot." Certainly the patristic disapproval of the curious, murky, dim, and mysterious world of tattoo is not entirely without reason. All too many tattoo artists have had criminal records of one kind or another. They have been drunks, winos, fences, dope-pushers, or scalawags of various sorts. Eyes a-gleam with the prospect of a fast and easy buck, they have tattooed underage boys; or have had them sign cards saying that they have permission for a tattoo from "Father" — a life-sized dummy in the shop corner, which by its silence gives consent. Some of them have been rightly accused of selling marijuana or worse. And the dirty, ill-lighted shops of many of the old-timers, with their aura of general evil, have been hardly conducive to making the patristic observers think of the artists as reputable citizens.

But in the larger cities, the old-timers are disappearing. The new shops of the younger group are models of sanitation. The needles gleam, the working areas are spotless, the autoclaves are actually used, the needle-bars are autoclaved and stored in sterile sealed paper envelopes, the tiny capsules are used for pigments, rubber gloves are worn, and great care in all the aspects of antisepsis are taken. But for the patrists, there is still something evil and wrong about the entire affair. The old rumors linger on, perpetuated by the cheap men's magazines and tabloids; even the modern articles in medical journals seem to carry on the old accusations about tattooing, and the doctors apparently know nothing of the way that many of the artists have policed themselves and adopted the best medical methods for sterilization.

Still, here and there about the country, mainly in rural areas, you can go into a tattoo shop and find an old-timer dipping into the large "community pot" of pigments, rinsing the needles in nothing but clear water, using the same "paint-rag" over and over to wipe the needle-ends, and a community sponge to wipe the tattoo after it is finished. If legislation against tattooing becomes universal, it will be the fault of the tattoo artists themselves, and their lackadaisical conformity to sterile techniques, or their deliberate rejection of such methods because they are too much trouble.

The mystery, the "otherness" of the tattoo world, are things for which many of the artists themselves are responsible. They sometimes deliberately cloud the nature of their work in order to create the mystique to justify their often exorbitant prices. More, they sense the disapproval of the patristic element, and are continually giving out tales calculated to raise the profession to a socially acceptable level, like the late Tatts Thomas in Chicago, who archly claimed to do most of his work in hospitals . . . on eyeballs.

A tattoo artist finds it difficult to consider his occupation objectively. If he did, intelligently, he might be the first to admit the practice *is* primitive, barbarous, and out of place in a theoretically enlightened civilization. To put a colored design under the skin — is this not something which we associate with savage tribal practices rather than with a computer society which can send men to the moon?

On the other hand, is tattooing any more barbarous than piercing the ears to wear ear-rings, putting rings on fingers, red lacquer on toes and fingernails, rouge on cheeks, colors on eyelids, dyes on hair? If those quaint habits are all matters of personal taste and preference, then so is the decoration of the skin with tattoos. It would hardly seem to involve morality or law at all; certainly it would not, if one considers the etymology of the word "morality" — from *mos, mores* — meaning the customs of the people, the things they *actually* do, rather than those which they pretend to do, or the precepts and laws which they pretend to follow.

There is something almost terrifyingly personal about the tattoo. How it seems to the customers I will never know, not even by empathic projection, but it was always satisfying to me while I was doing it. Sailors came back just to gossip, or to show me the way their tattoos turned out. I gave them a brush for their wool uniforms, I let them sew buttons on, I tied their ties if as boots they had not yet learned how. And finally, there was the gratification of being my own man, taking no orders from pudgy deans, having a place of my own.

Moreover, where in the world, or in what job, could you have someone tell you a story like this?

A young kid came in, a borderline eighteen-year-old. I asked him what high-school he attended, and he mentioned a Catholic one, so that I was sure he was too young to have a tattoo. And then he went on:

"I was in the corridor oncet," he said, "when a Sister saw the edge of my tattoo under my short-sleeve shirt. She took one finger and lifted the sleeve up and said, kinda severe, 'Is that a real tattoo?' and I said 'Yeah, Sister,' expectin' to get the hell bawled outen me. She looked at it for about a minnit, and then sorta cocked her head to the side funny-like, and said, 'You know, I almost got one of those in Frisco myself oncet.'"

Appendix A
A Brief Historical Sketch of Tattooing

The origins of tattooing are as shrouded in mystery and speculation as are the motivations to get tattooed. Perhaps the instinct to be decorated has always existed, from the period of pre-history down to the present.

Unquestionably, the earliest tattoos had magical or ritual significance, and were presumed to have powers to protect or heal. In the primitive mind, excoriations, scarifyings, and cuttings were able to release demons from the body and to cure illness of various kinds. But as for tattoos, no scholar of prehistory can do much more than surmise, or attempt a reconstruction from the various hints that are available. If red or blue dyes were found in the Egyptian tombs of 4000 B.C., or those of the Natuf culture even earlier (9000-600 B.C.), are we then to presume that the body was marked with these, or did they serve another purpose?

One of the best modern scholarly and anthropological treatises is the volume by D.W. Hambly, *The History of Tattooing and Its Significance (1925)*. In this monumental investigation, Hambly states that any inquiry into the origin of the practice will take the investigator far beyond the narrow confines of 6,000 years of recorded history. Archaeologists claim that studies of the Stone Age in the period around 12,000 B.C. have revealed evidence of marks or cuttings made upon the bodies, and have deduced that ritual scars, some of them bone-deep, began very early to assume recognizable patterns.

But tattooing by puncture, as it is known today, with the insertion of a dye or pigment into the skin, seems to be definitely traceable to ancient Egypt. George Burchett in his *Memoirs of a Tattooist* (London, 1958) in an historical note says that he has seen tattoo marks on Egyptian clay dolls in the Ashmolean Museum at Oxford. And Hambly goes farther, stating that there exists positive archaeological proof that body marks by the puncture method were applied to human beings between 4000-2000 B.C. in Egypt, basing his conclusions on the marks on mummies.

Hambly attempts to trace the world progress of tattooing, which like a mysteriously surfacing and disappearing river, appears and vanishes throughout recorded history. Between 2800 and 2600 B.C., when the pyramids of Gizeh were being built, Egypt seems to have passed on the practice to Greece, Persia, Arabia, and Crete. By 2000 B.C. the art had spread throughout southern Asia to the Ainus, the ancient inhabitants of Japan, who probably adopted it and advanced it to a fairly high level. When the Ainu originally crossed the sea to Japan they brought tattooing with them, which they regarded as a divine gift endowed with all kinds of magical properties. Later, when the ancestors of today's Japanese settled the islands, they too adopted tattooing, but divested it of its magical status and turned it into an ornamental art alone. Thence it traveled to Burma, where it achieved the high degree of perfection it retains to this day, becoming even more strongly associated with religious and magical beliefs.

From Japan, Hambly continues, the wandering trail of tattooing moved southwards around 1200 B.C. to the Philippines, Borneo, Formosa, and the South Sea Islands.

How the practice ever reached the ancient Scythians, however, spreading northwards over what is now Russia, is a question best left to conjecture. Herodotus visited the Scythians in the fifth century B.C., and described and memorialized them. An article in *Natural History: The Journal of the American Museum of Natural History* (New York, October 1960) entitled "The Royal Scythians," describes their tattoos in detail. The designs were fascinating and impressive. This is precisely known, since one of their "princely tombs," preserved by glacial ice over the centuries, yielded the body of a man with the tattooing still intact and perfect on his preserved skin. It was quite elaborate, an excellent example of the "animal style" with which the Scythians decorated their golden vessels and artifacts, collections of which were made by Peter the Great in 1763, when the first Scythian caches were found.

In that same fifth century B.C., tattooing on its southward voyage reached the Polynesians, who occupied many of the South Sea

Islands in their spreading migrations; and the art eventually reached what is now New Zealand. There the natives developed the "Moko" style, intricate patterns of tattooing associated with religious rites and taboos. These Moko tattoos are still created among the Maoris and the inhabitants of some of the southern islands, and were always applied in accordance with ceremonial regulation — different patterns identifying tribal communities, rank, families, virgins, and married women.

To turn briefly eastward, the arrival of tattooing in the Americas is still an enigma to the anthropologists. The people of Peru and Mexico somehow knew of it, and the later high civilizations of the Incas, Aztecs, and Mayans made important religious and ritualistic use of it. Some authorities are of the opinion that the Polynesians introduced it to these countries on their trans-Pacific voyages; others surmise that the Siberians (possibly the Scythians) crossed by land and sea to Alaska, and working south, initiated the North American tribes into the art. Aside, however, from the original scarifications and cuttings, with the possible introduction of soot (which did not stay in the skin well) into the cuttings, the North American Indians never got very far with the insertion of pigments under the skin. Anthropologists have theorized that the Indians used vegetable dyes which were rather quickly absorbed and "digested" by the body; and at last, tiring of this, the Indians reverted to — or rather invented — the idea of war-paint, which was simply applied to the surface of the skin.

Another branch of the trail of tattooing evidently left Egypt and wandered north into Europe. The Iberians, preceding the Celts into the British Isles, were great practitioners of the art, as were the Picts of Scotland, the Gauls, and the invading Teutonic races. Farther to the west and later, the Romans practiced it to mark slaves and criminals instead of hot brandings; and even earlier, Herodotus recounts its use in the Greek wars, telling the story of the slave whose head was shaved and inscribed with a secret message. His hair was then allowed to grow and he was sent to the receiver who shaved the slave's head and read the message. In these days of instant communication by satellite, such a method would arrive long after the war had ended.

When the Danes, Norsemen, and Saxons invaded England and

found the custom of tattooing there, they adopted it for themselves, but brought advances in the artistry; they enjoyed their family crests and tribal symbols tattooed upon themselves.

Before Christianity came, the Israelites (3500-1500 B.C.) developed the custom of putting markings and/or cuttings on their hands and arms when a relative died. This custom decreased around 1250 B.C. and was formally interdicted by the pronouncement in Leviticus 19.28. But the Jews evidently did not follow the prohibition very faithfully, for believers often had the *tau* (which later became the "cross of Anthony") tattooed on their foreheads as a protective sign. The association of this with the "mark of Cain" (inscribed so that Cain would be kept alive to suffer for his crime) is a matter of fascinating speculation.

The many references to "bearing in my body the marks of the Lord" which are to be found in the New Testament, particularly in the Apocalypse or the Book of Revelation, have already been considered in the text above. According to one statement, the world will not be destroyed before 144,000 Israelites, twelve thousand from each tribe, have tattooed a cross on their foreheads or right hands, so that they will be able to enter a better life. One is tempted to remark that in view of the Orthodox prohibition against tattooing, the world may be safe for a long time to come; evidently the tattooed numbers on Holocaust victims were overlooked by someone with a finger on the button.

An examination of the pertinent passages in the Talmud and elsewhere (by such scholars as ben Nappacha, Buxtorf, and others) has suggested one of the oddest possibilities of all—that Jesus Christ himself was tattooed. In the Talmud and elsewhere it has been claimed that Christ practiced Egyptian magic, but was never allowed to speak or write of it; and that he tattooed the magic word for Jehovah [Yahweh] on his thigh, as well as made incisions in his skin while in the House of the Sanctuary.

But Christianity stopped the "barbarous practice" of tattooing at least for a while, and set up the prejudice against it which has existed ever since the Ecumenical Council of Nicaea in 787 A.D., during which Pope Hadrian I declared a ban against it. Thus by "negative proof" it may be considered to have become quite popular among priests and people, since no law is ever made unless it be against a practice which has already been firmly established and widely followed. A succession of papal bulls was necessary during the following centuries to reinforce the ban. In the monastic chronicles of the 12th to 16th centuries, no mention whatever is made of tattooing. It must have been very hard on the military of the innumerable wars that ravaged Europe to be denied their skin-souvenirs of their conflicts, but of course if they had never heard of tattooing, they did not miss it much.

Despite the prohibitions from Rome, the art survived in Britain. King Harold and many of the early Anglo-Saxon kings before him were heavily tattooed. Perhaps the missionaries from Rome, reaching that backward country, felt that nothing could or should be attempted with the natives, who in the early years after England was Christianized still clung fiercely to their own customs. After the Norman invasion of 1066, however, nothing was heard of tattooing for many hundreds of years, although the body of King Harold II—killed in the battle of Hastings—was said to have been identified by the name of his wife tattooed above his heart.

The Judeo-Christian interdicts, then, and the Norman Conquest, thus gradually turned the British Isles away from tattooing; and still further disdain arose because of the tales which reached the "civilized" country of Britain, tales of painted wild men from Africa. Columbus, Cortez, and Pizarro brought tattooed prisoners back from the Americas. The fact that some of the Inca prisoners were tattooed branded them as savages in British eyes, where *le snobisme* was already being developed, even though the Incan and Mayan civilizations were at that time thought to be much higher than the European.

In most of Europe, tattooing enjoyed neither the artistic perfection it did in Japan, nor its popularity in the Americas. Oddly enough, during the 17th and 18th centuries, it was the Greek Catholic and Orthodox churches which kept tattooing alive, and even today many priests of the Coptic church are tattooed. Religious designs on chest or forearm have been traditional for two centuries with the Orthodox Bulgarians and Servians.

The word *tattoo* is of much more recent invention than the art itself, having been introduced by Captain James Cook in the narrative of his first principal voyage around the Horn and the Cape of

Good Hope (compiled by J. Hawkesworth from the journals of Cook and his botanist Joseph Banks, and published in London in 1773). Captain Cook used the word *tattaw*, deriving it from the Tahitian "ta" which in several Polynesian languages meant to *knock* or *strike*.

> They staine their bodies by indentinges, or pricking the skin with smalle instruementes made of bone, cutte into short teethe; which indentinges they fille uppe with dark-blue or blacking mixture prepared from the smoke of an oily nutte . . . This operation, which is called by the natives *tattaw*, leaves an indelible marke on the skin . . .

After his second voyage "towardes the Southe Pole and Around the Worlde," Cook told the British public even more about the rediscovered art, reporting on "the beautiful circles, crescents, and ornamentes" with which the natives decorated their bodies, and saying also that some designs represented dogs, birds, and men.

Even earlier than Captain Cook, William Dampier — a British buccaneer, sailor, and explorer — had returned in 1691 with a "Painted Prince" named "Jeoly" or "Gioli," according to Burchett. Dampier exhibited the Prince publicly in Britain to the great fascination of the audiences of William and Mary. And even the great Doctor Johnson, according to Boswell, went to see the tattooed native Omai, whom Cook brought back after his second voyage.

Hanns Ebenstenn in a charming and highly sympathetic small work (Ebenstenn is not a practitioner) entitled *Pierced Hearts and True Love* (London, 1953) says that Joseph Cabri, a Frenchman, appears to have been the first European to have been thoroughly tattooed in the primitive manner. He was exhibited publicly and caused a great stir, but died in poverty in Valenciennes in 1816. And shortly before the French Revolution a Paris advertisement referred to a sailor with "beautiful designs covering the whole body." By this time the rediscovered art had become popular with many sailors, especially those who had traveled to the islands of the Pacific.

In 1828 a Bristol mariner shocked and fascinated the British public with a tale of his having been captured by the Maoris who had forcibly tattooed him and kept him captive for six years. They compelled him to marry the chieftain's daughter, and after his initiation into the tribe by tattooing, the treatment he was accorded was quite pleasant; he was considered a person of distinction and an equal with the Maoris. The fact that his story was later exploded did not seem to upset the Britons at all.

From that point onward, tattooing was anyone's racket. The idea of "forcible tattooing" seemed to provoke more excitement than that which was done voluntarily, and one of the greatest fakirs was an Albanian named Alexandrinos, who became known in the United States as Prince Constantine. P.T. Barnum found him and together they concocted a story: that Constantine had been forcibly tattooed over all his body, even his face, by "Chinese Tartars" in Burma when captured, he alone surviving of his two (or was it three?) companions; he and Barnum could never make up their minds. Constantine was covered with hundreds of designs of small animals, the soles of his feet excepted. He was widely exhibited over all the world, making a good deal of money for Barnum; it is said that in the early 1900s his salary was $1000 a week, which would be munificent in the present day. I fell heir to what was said to be one of the animals cut from his body when he died in the 1920s—a brownish, dried, and possibly tanned gruesome little relic, but it was stolen from my Chicago shop by some aficionado who needed it more than I did.

The first professional tattoo artist in the United States is said to be one Martin Hildebrandt, who arrived in Boston in 1846 and established himself as a full-time practitioner of the art. During the Civil War (according to his reminiscences published in 1870 in New York), Martin tattooed soldiers of both sides, crossing freely between the lines and being welcomed royally by members of both armies. Thus doth art transcend the dogs of war.

To the end of the 19th century, all tattooing was done by hand, with needles tied into the end of a small stick in the Oriental manner, something like a pen-holder. But it is claimed that in 1891 the electric tattoo machine was patented by a British tattooist, Tom Riley (although Charlie Wagner of New York is said by one authority to have patented it a few years earlier), and after that there was no stopping the spread of the "art." From that day until 1962, no improvement was made in the basic design of the machine, although in that year a German tattooist named Horst Streckenbach invented a radically different tattoo-pen, with each instrument containing its own small motor to which was attached an irregular cam-wheel that furnished the up-and-down movement. This machine was never widely used.

In the United States tattooing reached a peak of popularity in the early 1900s, but after World War I there was a gradual decline, as the reputations of the tattoo artists sank downwards and public taste changed. The entrance into the game of con-men, winos, and ex-convicts and the degeneration of the tattoo "salons" and "surgeries" (as Burchett termed his) into the "joints" with sawdust and spittle on the floor, gave it an extremely bad name. And in the United States from 1920 on, the puritan element began to disapprove. Great artists like Britain's Sutherland Macdonald and George Burchett gave way to inept non-artists and hacks, "jaggers," carnival and circus operators who by no stretch of semantics could be called artists. The nexus of criminality and tattooing began to be stressed by those who were sure that a tattoo made a man a criminal, instead of the other way around—but the Little Old Ladies and the falwells could not see that. To the great disgrace of the *Encyclopedia Britannica*, it retains to this day a cross-reference from the word "Tattoo" to the semantically biased and slanted article on "Mutilations, Deformations, and Mayhem."

Gone are the days when the New York "400" thought it fashionable and daring to enhance the ankle of a debutante with a small rose. By 1962 the do-gooders and the falwells had made tattooing illegal or restricted it in thirty-two states to those above twenty-one years of age; by 1968 over 47 major cities also had special ordinances against tattooing. Circuses and carnivals now seldom include a tattoo artist among their personnel. With TV in the home, the moving pictures on Daddy's back are no longer needed. But after the survivors crawl from their caves in the years following the three hours of World War III, who can say whether they will not have passed their troglodyte days in the dark by collecting a little soot from their burning fat-pots, and using the last needle and safety-pin they can find to put the outline of a mushroom cloud on each other's arms? For the impulse to mark, to decorate, to memori-alize is older by far than recorded history—and the tribal laws of the New Primitive Society may not condemn it—at least until some time later.

Appendix B
A Note on the Literature of Tattooing

It is extremely difficult to find one's way through the literature of tattooing, and to separate the professional writing—usually medical or sociological—from that which has a more general appeal, and yet does not engage in sensationalism.

A very large bibliography is to be found appended to an early study made on the subject by Albert Parry in his book entitled *Tattoo* (New York, 1933). This bibliography is retrospective, multilingual, and all-inclusive to its date of publication; it includes works in English, Arabic, Dutch, French, German, Italian, and Spanish. Most of the works listed are too specialized for the general reader with only a casual interest in the subject, or else they are "fugitive" pieces which have appeared in publications no longer in existence, most of which would be found only in very large libraries, and often so rare that a would-be reader would have to present scholarly credentials to see them. Even so ambitious a listing of works is surpassed by the bibliography at the end of the volume by C. Bruno of Paris, entitled *Tatoués, qui êtes vous?* (Paris, 1974). It is evident to anyone who reads either of these volumes that the authors were not equipped to make use of so many languages in their own listings, nor does what they have to say indicate any acquaintance with the books they mention. This does not prevent either volume, however, from being lively and entertaining, and reasonably accurate, free from much of the balderdash and old wives' tales surrounding tattooing.

Parry's volume is more easily available to one who reads English only, if you can convince the rare book librarian that you will not slice out the color plates. It is very difficult to find a copy of this book at the present time; the price today might be prohibitive.

Parry, writing in 1933, was one of the first devotees of Freud, and was the first to apply the "new" Freudian terminology to tattooing. He interviewed a vast number of tattooists then alive, and like many journalists, accepted the tales they told him without any attempt at verification. His book so infuriated the few tattoo artists literate enough to read it and understand what he was saying that one and all denounced him for doing their art a great disservice. The fact remains that time has proved a large number of Parry's conclusions to be sound, and his book remains a milestone in the general literature of tattooing.

Since 1933, very little writing of importance has appeared in English. There has been only one volume (ghost-written for a practicing tattoo artist in Britain by Peter Leighton) of reminiscences by the late George Burchett, *Memoirs of a Tattooist* (London, 1958). This is also an amusing and entertaining volume to read, although it is to be taken with much salt, since Burchett was doing his best to upgrade the art, and his [pretended] disapproval of the true picture of what goes on is reminiscent of almost every tattooist's similar attempts. Of particular interest is Burchett's account of the tattooing he did on Frederik IX, king of Denmark, as lively and absorbing as Boswell's account of the meeting of Johnson and his King is fascinating. The volume is highly slanted in Burchett's favor, who styled himself "King of Tattooists."

Still available in libraries is D.W. Hambly's *The History of Tattooing and its Significance* (London, 1925; New York, 1927), the soundest and most scholarly of all works in English. Hambly was an anthropologist, and his main interest lies in the historical, sociological, and anthropological aspects of the practice. His work is highly theoretical and technical, and almost beyond the capabilities of the lay reader. It contains no account of modern tattooing, or at the most very inconsequential references, confining itself to the ancient history of tattooing and its origins. His bibliography reflects this. It is not recommended for the general reader.

A very pleasant small book is Hanns Ebenstenn's *Pierced Hearts and True Love* (London, 1958). It is not an accurate nor truly revelatory work but rather a sympathetic tribute to the art by a non-practitioner fascinated by the subject. It is filled with interesting photographs as well as some primitive line drawings — a book to charm and propagandize, rather than to enlighten and inform; it is an interesting introduction to the subject.

Another book in French has gained quite a reputation; it specialized in tattooing done in the French underworld and in prisons. This is *Le Tatouage du 'Milieu'* by Jacques Delarue and Robert Giraud (Paris, 1950). This is a study of hand-applied amateur tattooing in prison and among the people of the French underworld. What makes it especially interesting is the large number of photographs of crude "hand-jobs" done by prisoners, plus the line-drawings of gang-markings and anti-social designs traced by Delarue. The drawings and photographs in this book have been widely stolen and reproduced over the entire world, resulting in such sensational drivel as a small book pirated from Delarue's, entitled *Tattooed Women and Their Mates*, which barely mentioned women.

The best works in German, according to Horst Streckenbach of Frankfort, are two in number—one by Wilhelm Joest, entitled *Tätowieren, Narbenzeichnen und Körperbemalen* (Berlin, 1887), large format with many excellent illustrations. It does not emphasize the sexual aspects of tattooing to a great extent, but clearly indicates that tattooing is related to the sexual side of life. The other best one is by Adolf Spamer, *Die Tätowierung in den deutschen Haienstädten* (Bremen, 1934). In it are described all the tattoo shops in the German harbor towns at the time of the book's appearance. Shortly after Spamer's work appeared, all tattoo shops were closed by a special order from Hitler except one in Hamburg, and its owner had to sign a declaration that he would tattoo foreigners only—since tattooing did not meet with the dictator's approval, marking as it did the "pure, unblemished Aryan skin." Spamer's work is very detailed, filled with information and shedding much light on the meaning of sexual designs. His work is perhaps the best and most detailed work on tattooing in the German language up to the present.

For those more interested in the esoteric, a book by Luedecke, called *Erotische Tätowierungen* (Anthropophyteia Bd 4: Leipzig, 1925) deals mainly with erotic meanings of tattoos, especially as they were to be found on pimps, prostitutes, and the lower social class in general. Luedecke, however, evidently garnered most of his information from persons who found themselves in trouble with the law. The book is neither good nor bad from the point of view of the truth about tattooing, but for the year 1925 it must be considered quite excellent, with many good photographs.

A book (ghost-written by Mario Vassi for a tattooist named Spider Webb) entitled *Pushing Ink: The Fine Art of Tattooing* (New York, 1979) contains many inaccuracies and generalizations, but is nonetheless amusing to read if not taken too seriously. It presents much of the bizarre thinking and second-hand "philosophy" of the flower-children of the 1960s, especially to be noticed in the wild idea of the thousand Xs — although this is not necessarily more outré than the "thousand points of light" remark made by a high government official. It is in actuality a superior kind of picture book, copiously illustrated with many photographs and line-drawings, and sixteen pages in full color.

One unusual book entitled *The Tattooists*, privately published by Albert Morse (San Francisco, 1977) contains photographs of about a hundred tattooists together with brief snippets of comments from many of them; it does not to any great extent illuminate the subject of tattooing, but it has some value as a primary source, and is an interesting curiosity as a coffee-table book.

It is virtually impossible and pointless to attempt to trace the sensationalized articles produced in American magazines since 1940. Most of these popular articles are to be found either in so-called "men's" magazines, or "girlie" magazines. Aside from a very few of these articles, no true picture is ever to be obtained from them, either of tattooing or of tattoo artists. All to be found therein are the dangers of tattooing and its possibilities of infection — the same old myths which have been told and recopied in hundreds of instances. Most of them are completely worthless, drawn from the tales that the interviewers were told by the tattoo artists themselves, and comment has already been made about the unreliability of such information. Almost all of the articles condemn tattooing in the most puritanical, hypocritical, and falwellian traditions. A few may start out to sound sympathetic, but are eventually drawn into perpetuating the usual tired old falsehoods and the well-worn stories.

The very early investigative work on tattooing by Lombroso, Lacassagne, and others, all of the late 1800s, has been thoroughly discredited, and suffers from the lack of the scientific and psychiatric approach, simply because such an approach was hardly possible then. What they had to say is no longer acceptable in the light of modern science, scholarship, and investigation. Even such a modern scholarly article in French as that by Professor Jean Graven,

Dean of the Faculty of Law at the University of Geneva in Switzerland, entitled "Le Tatouage et sa Signification Criminologique," in two parts in the *Revue Internationale de Criminologie et de Police Technique* (vols. 13-14, 1959-60) smells so much of the lamp and the scholar's detachment that from a practical point of view it is nearly worthless. It may be entirely possible that Professor Graven never talked to a single tattooed criminal in his life, nor even saw one.

Several attempts have been made to start various magazines devoted entirely to tattooing. Most notable of these is one *Tattootime*, started in 1982 with D.E. Hardy as editor, containing interesting and often thought-provoking articles relating to such topics as the new tribalism, tattooing and magic, and others, printed on good quality stock with some color illustrations.

An extraordinarily bizarre book entitled *Modern Primitives* (Re/Search Publications, #12, 1989) contains many examples of modern tattooing and the practices of multiple piercings and ritual scarification. Its most valuable sections are those devoted to Don Ed Hardy and one or two other tattoo artists, but most of the work is anecdotal and reminiscent of many of the old-fashioned fads and fancies of the 1960s. Its scholarship is extremely suspect and its presented oddities quite dangerous for the novice to imitate. From its cover information: "'Primitive' actions which rupture conventional confines of behavior and aesthetics are objectively scrutinized. In context of the death of global frontiers, this volume charts the territory of the last remaining underdeveloped source of first-hand experience: *the human body*."

Dr. C.A. Tripp has very kindly furnished me with a thirty-page printout of the abstracts of 66 so-called "learned and scientific" papers published during the last twenty-five years in scientific journals of many languages in the Library of Congress. His comment was that these papers were very primitive, and indeed they seem no more than that, confining their remarks about the causes of persons getting tattooed to broken homes, criminal behavior, dope and such like—making the usual superficial confusions between cause and effect. Most of these articles really throw no new light at all on the subject of tattooing.

Aside from most of the books and writings mentioned in this

brief note, all of the other writing is quite likely to be theoretical, unreliable, and suspect. Tattooing is the one subject that—to be written about—demands a plunge into the waters, not a comfortable observer's beach-chair at the side of the ocean.

Index